Sunshine
for the
Latter-day
Saint
Mother's
Soul

Sunshine for the Latter-day Saint Mother's Soul

EAGLE GATE

SALT LAKE CITY, UTAH

Library of Congress Cataloging-in-Publication Data

Sunshine for the Latter-day Saint mother's soul.
    p.   cm.
Includes bibliographical references.
ISBN 1-57345-628-4 (pbk.)
    1. Mothers—Religious life. 2. Mormon women—Religious life. I. Deseret Book Company.
BX8641 .S86 2000
248.8'431'088283—dc21

99-86857

Printed in the United States of America

54459-6630

10   9   8   7   6   5   4   3   2   1

Contents

Husbands and Fathers

Struggle and Sacrifice

On the Lighter Side

An Eternal Perspective

$\mathscr{P}$reface

In an April 1997 conference address in which he paid tribute to mothers, Elder Jeffrey R. Holland observed, "The work of a mother is hard, too often unheralded work." He went on to say: "Mothers, we acknowledge and esteem your faith in every footstep. Please know that it is worth it then, now, and forever. . . . If you try your best to be the best parent you can be, you will have done all that a human being can do and all that God expects you to do" ("'Because She Is a Mother,'" *Ensign,* May 1997, pp. 35, 36).

Such words of recognition and assurance can often be just what the Latter-day Saint mother needs to help sustain and motivate her in her important and demanding role. In the spirit of offering similar encouragement—as well as just plain reading pleasure—this collection of stories and poems has been created for mothers in the Church and also for others who fill "mothering" roles.

As with previous volumes in the *Sunshine for the Latter-day Saint Soul* series, a hallmark of this compilation is its variety. There is something here to fit almost any mood or need. Looking for an inspirational story about a mother's faith, influence, or love? You'll find plenty of such stories in the sections devoted to those topics. Other themes addressed include children, husbands and fathers, struggle and sacrifice, and teaching moments. Maybe what you need to give your day a boost is a little chuckle. Go to the section called "On the Lighter Side" for some stories that will give you something to smile about.

With contributions from such mainstay authors as Ardeth G. Kapp, Elaine Cannon, Kathleen "Casey" Null, Marion D. Hanks,

Harold B. Lee, Patricia T. Holland, Michaelene P. Grassli, George D. Durrant, Anita R. Canfield, and Janene Wolsey Baadsgaard, *Sunshine for the Latter-day Saint Mother's Soul* will surely be a source of gladness, wisdom, and inspiration that you can draw from again and again.

The publisher expresses gratitude to the authors whose works make up this volume. Special thanks are also extended to Lesley Taylor for her help in selecting, compiling, and arranging the stories and poems included herein.

Motherhood:
A Divine Role

"*It* Never Gets Better Than This"

ARDETH G. KAPP

One evening more than twenty years ago, standing at the bedside of my three-year-old niece, Shelly, I pondered: When does the preparation for motherhood really begin? When do mighty souls become great mothers? What of the space between here and there?

At that time, I penned these few lines concerning that memorable experience and my unanswered questions: "All her other dolls had been lined up with care and placed aside. But at the close of the day when all was quiet, clutched in the bend of a fat little elbow was Sweetypie. Sweetypie had all the hair worn off the back of her head; one eye was missing, and one arm was almost detached. Yet there she was, tucked protectively under the arm of three-year-old Shelly. Standing in the twilight with the last rays of sun filtering through the shades, I looked long and thoughtfully at the quiet little girl now at rest from play. Almost reverently I rearranged the covers as I bent down to feel both her warmth and that of Sweetypie. At that moment I thought I was witnessing the beginning of a miracle, and I marveled at the beauty I saw. When is the season for gathering, acquiring, and developing? What of those attributes, skills, characteristics, and spiritual promptings that all become a part of the greatness? When do all the qualities of motherhood, the myriad bits and pieces and combinations of beauty, come together? When does the divine kaleidoscope take final form, so that no matter which way it turns or which parts are exposed, the pattern will enrich those who encounter its beauty? Whence springs the spiritual reservoir from which all members of the family may one day partake? Surely

3

Sweetypie had some place in the marvelous beginning of this preparation. As I left Shelly tightly holding her treasure, I continued to ponder about the space between here and there."

Over the past twenty years as I have sought for a deeper understanding of this miracle God has placed within reach of every righteous woman—according to his time and purpose—an accumulation of insights, impressions, and awakenings has come to my mind. The past, the present, and the future, so close together, seem on occasion to be beyond reach of time. Shelly one day released Sweetypie from the safe place in the bend of her arm and set her on the shelf. Later the doll was tucked away in the closet and finally relegated to a box of childhood treasures in the basement. A season had ended. Shelly had outgrown, left behind, and even forgotten (or so she thought) the childhood joy she had felt with Sweetypie cradled in the bend of her arm.

We must let go of the past if we are to reach out to the unknown future with all its possibilities. For Shelly, it was in junior high that the excitement of the unknown became an ecstasy unexpected. She became a cheerleader. After one particularly exciting game finally won by her team, Shelly burst into the kitchen where her mom was waiting for her. "Oh, Mom!" Shelly exploded, jumping up and down, still filled with the excitement of the cheering crowd and the screaming thrill of victory. "Oh, Mom, it never gets better than this." Her mother, not wanting to be too casual about a moment so important to Shelly, smiled inwardly as she said tenderly, "Yes, Shelly, my dear, it does."

One season follows the next overnight, or so it seems. Years had flitted by, and the once excited cheerleader was now crowned high school homecoming queen. The cheering of the crowd was more personal this time. As Shelly rode in the parade, the people were calling her name. There was no mistaking the fact that the excitement was focused on her—it was even printed in the town paper. That night, when the shouting and the tumult had settled, Shelly sat on the bed by her mom and dad. "Oh, Mom, it never gets better than this!" Once again, with proper sensitivity to her young daughter's excitement, Shelly's mother responded, "Oh yes, my dear, it does."

Following more sunrises and sunsets, Shelly's tour to faraway places as a member of the Brigham Young University dance team brought applause that was translatable in every language. A postcard written home in a hurry exclaimed, "Mom and Dad, we are a real hit!" And then, perhaps remembering past times, but maybe not, Shelly scrawled a small postscript along the bottom of the card, "Mom, it never gets better than this," with a little smiley face to help carry the message. Her mom read the card and tucked it away to be used, perhaps, at some future date to confirm her answer not spoken, "Yes, Shelly, it does."

The bud must release its grasp if the flower is to bloom. With a sense of sacrifice, this young woman determined to leave the crowd and the applause and for eighteen months to fill a mission. Would it be worth it? she wondered. Could she ever come back to all of this? And yet she was drawn forward by a sense of purpose she did not fully understand at that time. From her mission in a far-off land, she wrote home regularly to report of the hard times and the good. Her parents watched for the letters with great anticipation. One day a letter came bearing a message across the top in bold strokes, "Oh, Mom and Dad, it never gets better than this." Pages of details followed about strangers who had become literally brothers and sisters in the gospel. Shelly loved them with a kind of love she had never experienced before. The sacrifice she was making to serve her mission was a small thing to pay in exchange for this new kind of joy. There were no crowds, no cheering, not even any applause, but rather a quiet testimony, tears of gratitude, and whispered expressions of love at the side of a baptismal font.

Another season and another time. In the temple on the glorious morning marked as her wedding day, while enveloped in her mother's arms, this little three-year-old who had so quickly blossomed now whispered in love and gratitude, "Oh, Mom, now I understand. It never gets better than this." Not wanting to lessen the joy of this grand experience, this event of eternal consequence, still her mother felt impelled to whisper, "Yes, my dear, it does."

Another year, in the quiet seclusion of a humble student apartment, it seemed that time stood still for a moment while generations looked on. A newborn babe nestled in that arm where Sweetypie had once claimed residence. As the baby took life nourishment from his mother's breast, his father expressed his own joy accompanying this drama, playing with great feeling a Chopin sonata on the piano. The new grandmother was on the scene to assist in this life-changing experience. Without taking her eyes from the miracle she held in her arms, and lacking adequate words to express her adoration and her joy, Shelly spoke in hushed tones, "Oh, Mom." Unable to restrain herself, her mother interrupted with the words she had waited for years to confirm, "You are right, my dear, it never gets better than this."

To Mother

ELAINE CANNON

From the children:
Touch me soft
Be gentle
Listen to me
Care
Let me see
Your eyes
So I will know
You're there.

From their father:
Touch me, love,
Be tender
Let me speak my
Part.
Bathe me
With your eyes, dear,
That I may know
Your heart.

From Heavenly Father:
Reach me now.
Be prayerful.
Let your spirit shine.
Seek me—
For the answers
To fill your heart
Are mine!

If This Is the Best Time, I Don't Want to Be Around for the Worst

JANENE WOLSEY BAADSGAARD

This is the best time of your life!" my elderly neighbor chuckled as I threw down the hose and raced to rescue my one-year-old, who was tumbling down the steps of our new home.

If one more person says that to me, I'm going to scream! I thought as I tried to comfort my crying baby and watched my two-year-old from the corner of one eye. I was four months pregnant with our third child and trying to keep our newly seeded lawn wet in hundred-degree weather.

"Your lawn's coming along fine," my elderly neighbor smiled as she walked toward me. Her face was dry and scented with cake powder. She seemed calm and composed. I was perspiring and trembling with frustration.

"How can you say that?" I asked. "I can't even see any grass for all those weeds. Sometimes I think that's all I ever do—water the weeds."

"Don't worry about the lawn," advised my neighbor. "You'll see. Pretty soon all this watering will pay off, and your grass will crowd out all those weeds. All new lawns are like this. But things will change." She waved as she walked back toward her house. "This is the best time of your life, dear."

Well, if this is the best, I thought, *I don't want to be around for the worst.*

I had decided older folks just didn't appreciate what they had. They could get up whenever they wanted. They had time to immerse themselves in music, literature, art—everything I didn't have time for.

Eating one meal without wanting to bring in the garden hose to wash down the kitchen and kids would have been the high point of my day. It seemed as though all I ever did was wash diapers, faces, walls, floors, clothes, or dishes. My hands looked like they hadn't been out of water in years. In the evenings, after the children were safely tucked in bed, I usually tried to fit in some writing, art, or music—but, more often than not, something else needed washing again.

Then, one morning, a concerned trip to the doctor brought warnings of a possible miscarriage and instructions for bed rest. The children were packed up and taken to my mother's. Suddenly I had all the time I longed for and all the bed rest I wanted. It was wonderful!

But as the days wore on, something strange happened. I started missing my water-dimpled hands. This "no-work-to-do" business was getting old in a hurry.

A week later, I was still resting and the miscarriage still threatened. Late one night, contractions began. My husband carried me to the car, and we drove to the hospital. Lying with my head in my husband's lap, I looked out the window into the black sky.

Later, at the hospital, the doctor advised me to be philosophic about the whole thing. "After all," he explained, "most women have a spontaneous abortion or two during their childbearing years."

I wanted to kick him in the teeth. The loss I felt was overpowering. My husband sat quietly at my side, his eyes red and tired.

Days later, at home, I sat outside on the porch with my two small daughters. I noticed that the lawn, after weeks of my absence, had really changed, just as my elderly neighbor had predicted. The small, tender green seedlings were growing into mature blades of grass. All my watering had paid off.

It occurred to me that perhaps all the work involved in caring for a young family was like our newly seeded lawn. It seems to be all work and water at first—and it's hard to see the tender seedlings beneath the weeds.

I knew then that if I didn't stop and look, I would miss something important. I would miss the joy in my children's growing. In time they, like the lawn, would not require my constant care. And the time would have passed all too quickly.

Perhaps, unlike my neighbor had suggested, this was not the best time of life. In fact, it might be no better or worse than any other time. But I would have this time only once—and if I missed the joy of growing in everything around me or within myself, I would truly miss it all.

From a New Mother

JEANETTE B. JARVIS

My child was born last night.
And since that hour my self-sufficient
Pride and will have fled.
The pow'r which once I felt within my grasp
Is humbled, in the wonder of it all—
This miracle, that mortals should have grace
To bring to earth a spirit—near divine.
Emotions, which were flaunted then so bold,
Have learned to loose their tears in quiet pain.
Compassion fills my soul for others' grief;
My fellow man is dearer than before.

This precious being, helpless in my arms,
Has turned my unskilled hands to trust in God . . .
And now my heart can pray.

My child was born last night—
And I, today.

"Therefore He Made Mothers"

HAROLD B. LEE

A family consisting of my grandmother, my mother, and two or three of the younger children were seated before an open door, watching the great display of nature's fireworks as a severe thunderstorm raged near the mountain where our home was located. A flash of chain lightning followed by an immediate loud clap of thunder indicated that the lightning had struck very close.

I was standing in the doorway when suddenly and without warning my mother gave me a vigorous push that sent me sprawling on my back out of the doorway. At that instant, a bolt of lightning came down the chimney of the kitchen stove, out through the open doorway, and split a huge gash from top to bottom in a large tree immediately in front of the house. If I had remained in the door opening, I wouldn't be writing this story today.

My mother could never explain her split-second decision. All I know is that my life was spared because of her impulsive, intuitive action.

Years later, when I saw the deep scar on that large tree at the old family home, I could only say from a grateful heart: Thank the Lord for that precious gift possessed in abundant measure by my own mother and by many other faithful mothers, through whom heaven can be very near in time of need.

During my young boyhood, there were many occasions when Mother's instructive and intuitive understanding prompted her to know that help was needed. Once on a stormy night she directed my father to go and search for me, only to find that my horse had stumbled and thrown me into a pool of half-frozen mud. My mother had known that help was needed.

Someone has coined a statement that has great significance: "God could not be everywhere, and therefore he made mothers."

Happy Mother's Day, Sweetheart

EILEEN GIBBONS

To a little girl with freckles and pigtails a mother is a queen and a goddess. She moves about, automatically being where she needs to be for the little girl's every wish, and she sort of unwinds like a clock, every tick representing something wonderful. She knows all the stories in the world, more, in fact, than all the schoolteachers combined, the answers to a myriad of unanswerable questions, and is beautiful besides.

Nothing unhappy ever happens to her because she is a mother. Laughter or tears, love or hate—all these seem apart from the mother whom the little girl worships.

As she goes into her teens, the girl also goes from pigtails to curls, effortlessly and automatically, of course. Mother can do everything. The girl realizes that her mother can cook, sew, and work hard—qualities more human than those she knew in her mother a few years ago—and without pathos the girl lets her mother do them. After all, she is a mother. Mothers are still wonderful, and they can do everything.

But when a girl, through one experience, then another, begins to mature, she gradually realizes that her mother is a "person"; that she isn't an automatic, unwinding, transfigured angel, or a bodiless, partless, passionless goddess—she can even make a mistake. A mother!

Dear Mother—ever since I discovered that you were a "person," that you actually thought, lived, laughed, and loved like others, that you were me in a few years and your mother a few years ago, I have had to form a new concept of a mother. I have lived with the growing realization which has formed this new concept for years now.

Like a child who is delighted with the Church because of Primary parties and fun in Sunday School, I as a child and teenager was delighted with you. And just as a few experiences in life teach us what the Church is really about, a knowledge that thrills us deeply, I have begun to realize what a mother really is, and I am in awe. Mother now is far more wonderful, far more a goddess and far more lovable as a human being than she was as something direct from the seventh heaven—because we expect miracles from the supernatural, but when humans perform them, that's something. And mothers do—every day! Think, Mother, of the millions of questions, tears, joys, and problems Mother is there to solve and understand.

Think of the many times in your life, Mother, the many times every day when your whole purpose has been helping the family, or friends, or the needy whom you don't even know. This purpose *is* your life, all your life.

For every washing, ironing, scrubbing, every sleepless night during sieges of mumps [and] rheumatic fever . . . , every meal prepared, whether it is bread and gravy or steak, for every prayer you have offered in behalf of others, for every unselfish deed of your whole life, you shall have a star in your crown. And you shall have a crown.

Yes, you are a "person." You, like all of us, can have stomach aches, bad days and bad nights. But, Mother, my dear, may you have very few more in the next fifty years. I wish that God would give you today, sort of in advance, the rest from all trouble, care and sorrow which he promises to people like you in the scriptures. (Alma 40:11–12.) You are on the right track. You are a good mother—helpful and loving. You and Daddy have had a material struggle providing for us, and it is a spiritual struggle to keep our thoughts always in harmony with His. But it is worthwhile, and we can receive unbounded aid from Him.

You know, Mother, even as you know you are reading this, that He is there, He is mindful of you, loves you and will help you in all you do. You have known that for as long as you can remember. . . .

Abundant love on another Mother's Day. May the days between now and the next one be joyous.

Love,
Eileen

A Parent's Reverie

SUSAN NOYES ANDERSON

"Who shall ascend into the hill of the Lord? or who shall stand
in his holy place?" (Psalm 24:3).

Sometimes when I am quite alone, and still,
The Spirit speaks, and whispers words of truth:
That I am not the master of your youth,
And was not called to bend you to my will.

I was not called to bend you to my will,
Nor would He have me bind you to His own.
His yoke is one that you must bear alone;
I cannot thirst for you, nor drink your fill.

I cannot thirst for you, nor drink your fill,
Though living water springs forth pure and sweet;
Yet I can but direct your wand'ring feet,
For you must tread the path and climb the hill.

For you must tread the path and climb the hill
That leads you back into His warm embrace.
I see you standing in His holy place,
Sometimes when I am quite alone, and still.

The Issue Was Simple

PATRICIA T. HOLLAND

As a young law professor, Elder Dallin H. Oaks was closely associated with Supreme Court Justice Lewis M. Powell. Justice Powell's daughter was herself a recent graduate of a fine law school, following which she began a successful law practice and a marriage almost simultaneously. Some time thereafter she had her first child. In paying a courtesy call as a family friend, Elder Oaks was pleasantly surprised to find this young mother at home with her child full time. When he asked about this decision, she replied, "Oh, I may go back to the law sometime; but not now. For me the issue was simple. Anyone could take care of my clients, but only I can be the mother of this child."

"Where Is My Mothers' Manual?"

LaDawn A. Jacob

Several years ago, my cousin Donna was a Gospel Doctrine teacher. The course of study that year was the Doctrine and Covenants. One morning, her husband, dressed for work in his immaculate, pressed suit, mentioned that he had an appointment for lunch with the stake president. Donna had put on her old work clothes, gearing up to manage their seven boys at breakfast. "You know," she said to her husband, "the Doctrine and Covenants is such a wonderful priesthood manual for men. I'm wondering, Where is my mothers' manual for handling these spirits that the Lord has entrusted to me?" As she later worked in her garden, this question kept returning. Finally she prayed, "Heavenly Father, where is the manual, the instruction booklet for me, for all mothers?" And the Spirit whispered to her, "Donna, I wrote it in your hearts."

Women have been blessed with the gift of inspired nurturing, entitling us to have his words written in our hearts to guide each of us in our individual stewardships.

A Mother's Love

other

JOSEPH F. SMITH

I learned in my childhood that no love in all the world can equal the love of a true mother. I am at a loss to know how it would be possible for any one to love children more truly than did my mother. I have felt, sometimes, How could even the Father love his children more than my mother loved hers? Her love was life to me, it was strength, encouragement; it was a love that begot love or likeness in myself. I knew she loved me with all her heart and soul. She would toil and sacrifice herself day and night for temporal comforts and blessings to provide for and give to her children. No sacrifice of self—of her time, leisure, pleasure, or opportunities for rest—was considered for a moment, when compared with her duty and love to her children.

When fifteen years of age, I was called to a foreign country to preach the gospel—or to learn how, and to learn it for myself. The strongest anchor of my life, which helped to hold my ambitions and desires steady, to bring me upon a level and keep me straight, was the love of my mother. Only a young boy, with immature judgment, without the advantages of an education, I was thrown into the midst of the greatest temptations possible for any boy or man to be subjected to. Yet, whenever those allurements became most enticing to me, the first thought that arose in my soul was this: "Remember the love of your mother. Remember how she strove for your welfare. Remember how willing she was to sacrifice her life for your good. Remember what she taught you in your childhood." Mother always insisted upon my reading the New Testament—the only book, except a few school books, that we had in the family, or that was within the reach of us at that time. My love for my mother and the recollection of her teachings became a strong defense, a protecting barrier between sin, temptation and me. I became able to turn aside from evil by the help of the Lord, and because of the love begotten in my soul toward her whom I knew loved me more than any other living being could love me.

A wife may love her husband, but this love is different from the love of mother for her child. The true mother, the mother who has the fear of God and the love of truth in her soul, will never hide from danger and harm, nor leave her child exposed to them. But, as naturally as sparks fly upward, and as it is to breathe the breath of life, mother steps between her child and danger. She will defend her child to the uttermost. Her life is as nothing in the balance, in comparison with the life of her child. That is the love of true motherhood—for children.

I place a high estimate upon the love of mother. I have often said, and will repeat it, that the love of a true mother comes nearer to being like the love of God than any other kind of love.

Thoughts Inspired by a Letter from a Daughter to a Mother

S. DILWORTH YOUNG

Sometime ago I said I
Loved you sixty ways
And counted them
To you.
But now I know I cannot
Count my love by
Any days.
My very breath is mine
Because you dared
To give your life that I might
Live.
Each day you gave to
Me that I might give
To mine
In my appointed time.
I cannot give to you
What you gave me
But to my own I pass
The torch
Then anxious, wait to
See
If they will pass to theirs
What you gave me.

The Journal

ELAINE CANNON

The teenage son was having trouble relating to his family. His thoughts and his behavior were cluttered with the onslaught of life that came at him as fast as the inches at the end of his legs. His mother's demands especially seemed a burden. He didn't know her anymore. He wasn't sure she understood him at all, and he was shocked to discover that after all she wasn't perfect as he had thought her to be when he was much younger. His older sisters were to him mere replicas of the authority figure he resented in his mother.

Then one day he came upon his mother's open journal. Reading it was a temptation he couldn't resist. A perfunctory glance or two, almost a sneer, and then quiet as he turned the pages that revealed a spiritual side to his mother he hadn't appreciated. Soon uncomfortable tears were burning his cheeks. He learned from this irrevocable source that his mother loved him. He also realized that she prayed for him and that she was mindful of good things he had done. Then he read a note tucked inside, written by one of his sisters for Mother's Day. He'd never suspected that she was capable of such deep feeling. He was interested in reasons she expressed for loving their mother, reasons that simply hadn't occurred to him. The warmth filling his heart opened a door in his mind. He hadn't understood. This record taught valuable lessons at the very time he needed to learn them. He gained new insights in all interfamily relating. He mellowed under the security of such a blessing and of being loved. In return, he felt love for others freshen his soul again. For him the world began all over again.

To My Son

KAYE R. ANDERSON

His sweet little hand wrapped tightly around my finger, just barely able to complete the circle. His grip was strong and very tight, but so soft. A tear slid down my face and landed on his rosy cheek as I held him close. I felt I could enjoy that moment forever. And I also felt I had so much time to enjoy him as he grew.

We walked together and played and worked. We had been a family for what seemed just a few moments, when he was walking along beside me hanging on to my hand. With his child's vocabulary he reminded me to slow down so his little short legs could keep up with my stride. We reached a puddle and I hopped over it. Reaching back, I took his chubby hand in mine, and with little effort I pulled him across.

We have shared many moments in just a few years. I have not changed; I have not grown older within my heart. Yet today I reached a puddle, and he reached out and took my hand in his large strong one, completely engulfing it with his grasp. And effortlessly he pulled me across. Now it is I who must ask him to slow down so I can keep up with his long stride.

As I look up into his strong and handsome face, I wonder now where the years have gone. They were but moments, and I wasted so many. Did I let him know how much I love him, and how proud I feel as he honors his priesthood?

I love you, son.

*Just What He Needed

BROOKIE PETERSON

A gift that women have is the ability to console.

One Sunday morning I was sitting in a large building where our stake conference session was soon to start. In front of me was a family with seven or eight children. The mother was at one end of the group; the father was near the other end. Farthest away from the mother was the next to youngest child—a boy about three years old. He was climbing on his chair when the seat started to close up, catching and pinching his leg. He started to howl; his father extricated him and tried to comfort him but was not particularly demonstrative as he did. The little boy screamed until he was lifted and passed from one brother or sister to the next. Finally he reached his mother, who held him close, kissed his tears, and cuddled him for several minutes. It was just what he needed. Soon the sun shone again and he was back down at the other end, laughing with his father.

I'm not implying that fathers can't console, but mothers—women in general—are usually much better at it because of their natural inclinations. Joseph Smith described these tendencies: "It is natural for females to have feelings of charity and benevolence" (*History of the Church,* 4:605).

The ability to nurture does not bring applause from the world, but because it tenderly lifts so many lives it is probably one of the most significant talents you have.

Why Does My Mother's Day Potted Plant Always Die?

JANENE WOLSEY BAADSGAARD

For a few weeks before Mother's Day, kids all over the country start wondering what to get Mom for her special day.

It's only right that children should wonder about their mothers for a few weeks a year. After all, mothers are wondering all year long about the kids. Moms all over the planet continually ask themselves, "Why is it that a child who forgets to do his homework, who can't even remember to flush the toilet, can remember exactly how much allowance *he* got when *he* was in the first grade?"

When a woman has her first baby, she becomes a mother. Easy enough. When she lets emotion overrule reason and has baby number 2, she suddenly becomes a referee, only she doesn't get to wear a striped shirt, blow a whistle, or control the game.

The moment baby number 2 is born, baby number 1 approaches Mother in the recovery room of the hospital with "The Sibling Bill of Rights." Mother will never fully recover because of it.

From this time on and forevermore, Mothers must count the M&M's to make sure each child gets exactly the same amount. For the rest of her mothering career, she is subjected to acute sibling attacks.

This strange malady works like this: If one child gets a present or treat or any personal attention, the other child immediately starts clenching his jaw muscles. His eyeballs flash red lasers and smoke shoots out his ears while a voice says, "Why is *his* ice-cream cone bigger than mine?"

This child cannot remember to bring his gym clothes home to get washed, but he can tell you exactly what Grandma gave him for his birthday when he was thirteen. Ask a child his multiplication facts and his mind may slip on one or two. But ask him whose turn it is to sit by the window in the car and you have bull's-eye accuracy.

The same child who is having trouble with measurement principles in math at school can tell you up to a micromillimeter who has the biggest piece of cake after supper. He can weigh bowls of cereal to see who got the most by balancing the bowls in both his hands while sticking out his tongue to test and allow for the wind factor.

There is really no way for Mother to win in this war. She began the losing battle when she allowed into her mind the naive thought, "Junior really needs a little brother to play with." From that point on, the only advantage she has in the fight is that she never has to employ spies.

"Mom! Jeff's been stuffing his dirty socks down the heat vents again!"

"Mom! Ann's hiding her snail collection in the toilet tank!"

Mothers never win. Just when you're finally starting to get used to waking up at 2:00 A.M. to feed the baby, the kid starts sleeping through the night. Just when you finally get diapering down to a science, the kid gets toilet trained. Just when you get really good at giving terrific birthday parties, the kid asks you to hide in your bedroom during his party so that you won't embarrass him in front of his friends. Just when your kid stops getting embarrassed when you come out of your bedroom, he moves away to go to college. By the time you finally know how to put on one heck of a wedding, all the kids are married off.

And don't be fooled. You can't pass along all that good stuff you learned when the kids have their own kids, because the in-laws think you're butting in where you're not invited if you give unsolicited advice. So you sit back and watch your kids make the same mistakes with their kids that you did with them, and you bite your tongue a lot.

Just when you think you're not going to worry about all this mother stuff anymore, one of the kids comes back home to stay and brings along a wife and seven kids.

On Mother's Day in church, people make you stand up and admit it. Then they give you a potted plant in perfect health, which you somehow always manage to kill in three days flat. You begin to wonder if the plant is somehow symbolic of your mothering abilities.

Always, without fail, someone will stand up in church on Mother's Day and say something like, "My mother never, oh, no, never, oh, not even one little time . . . raised her voice in our home."

You start to slink down in your seat and mumble something you hope no one can hear, but at the same time you want to jump up on your seat and scream, "What would she do if your pants were on fire?"

Before I became a mother, I always looked critically at other people's children and thought, "My children will never, no never, have unattended runny noses, limp bangs hanging in their eyes, or thumbs stuck disgustingly in their mouths." The other day I looked at my children. One had an unattended runny nose, one had limp bangs hanging in her eyes, and two others were disgustingly sucking their thumbs. Sometimes I wonder if maybe I should have been a nun.

When Rudyard Kipling wrote, "If you can keep your head when all about you are losing theirs and blaming it on you, if you can trust yourself when all men doubt you, but make allowance for their doubting too . . ." I think he had mothers in mind.

So while all the kids are wondering for a few short weeks what to get Mom for her special day, Mom is still, as always, wondering about the kids. No, she isn't wondering why she had you and your brother or sister. She's wondering why at one minute she feels such tenderness swell inside her, she can barely contain it without cradling you—then at another minute she hears herself yelling, "Why don't you grow up?"

She's wondering why after all the things she said that you

didn't listen to, you chose to listen to that one—"Grow up!"—and you did.

She knows the love she feels for you and your brother or sister is complete. She knows her love can't be divided up like a pie, with everybody getting a piece exactly the same size.

Every child gets the whole pie.

Mrs. Harrison

GLENN I. LATHAM

Several years ago, while doing some work in the Ogden, Utah, schools, I enjoyed the great blessing of working with two wonderful women, Mrs. Shaw and Mrs. Harrison, both elementary school teachers. As I observed them in their homes and in their classrooms, I was forever impressed by how sweet, gentle, kind, and "unflustered" they *always* were. They smiled and laughed. They encouraged and acknowledged appropriate behavior. They were everything I could ever hope parents and teachers would be.

One afternoon I was in the home of Mrs. Harrison where we were doing some planning relative to the project we were working on. She had to go to another room to get some materials, and as she walked past the overstuffed chair in which her youngest daughter was curled up reading a book, she gently ran her fingers across the girl's shoulders. Her daughter looked up and smiled. Mrs. Harrison looked back, winked, and smiled.

Later I said to Mrs. Harrison, "I'll bet you have a great relationship with your daughter." She replied, "Yes. She is a wonderful girl. I'm just very lucky." I hastened to note, "I suspect that luck has little or nothing to do with it."

$\mathscr{A}$ Homemade Sissy

GEORGE D. DURRANT

Dear Mom,

I really think I could have been a tough guy. You could have guaranteed that if you had spent more time with other people and less time with me. I wanted to be tough. You knew that, but you wanted me to be what we called in American Fork a "sissy."

You were always interfering in my life. You said that I was a good boy, yet at the same time you acted as if the world would come to an end if I didn't go to church. If I was so good, why couldn't you bear to see me miss church a few times? After all, church is a place to learn to be good, and you seemed to feel I was already good.

You were a soft woman, Mom. You weren't tough at all. I could get away with anything with you, as long as what I wanted to do was good. But let me try to do something tough, like I sometimes wanted to, and I could see a hurt look in your eyes. I couldn't stand to see that. Because of that kind of interference, I had to turn back to being a sissy.

Then there was that navy blue suit. It was all right to send for your dresses that were pictured in the Montgomery Ward catalog, but you really blocked me away from my tough-guy goals when you sent off to Denver for that double-breasted, navy blue suit.

I remember when it came. We unpacked it and I went in my bedroom and put it on. It fit perfectly, and when I came out I could see by the look in your eyes that I really looked good. I had a tie that you tied for me. Each week after church you told me to loosen the tie and pull it over my head so it would stay tied. That double-breasted suit wouldn't have done so much to keep me being a sissy except for the fact that even way back then I looked so good in navy blue.

When I'd pass the sacrament you would watch every move that I made. I could tell you wanted to stand up and shout, "See that boy right there, passing the sacrament, the one in the navy blue suit? That's my son. That's my George." If you hadn't been so reverent you'd have done that, wouldn't you, Mom?

Don't get me wrong. I didn't really mind the attention that you gave me. But was it really that big a thrill to have me dressed in my navy blue suit performing an errand for the Lord? Wouldn't some sort of public recognition for me or for you have been more fulfilling than that which we both privately felt in the chapel? Mom, don't cry, I was just asking.

People visiting in our home said, "Marinda, you sure do spoil that boy." I didn't know then what that really meant. Now, looking back, I know they were right. You really did spoil me. I think it was all part of your plan to keep me from being a tough guy. Nobody in history was ever as good to anyone else as you were to me. Seeing you, being near you, talking to you, was the center of all my happiness. My greatest boyhood fear was that I would lose you. So much of what I did that was good I did because I wanted to please you. So much of my regret came from the times I knew I had disappointed you.

I've seen people influencing other people, but none of what I've seen has ever equaled the influence you had on me. You didn't take any psychology classes at college and you didn't read any books on the problems faced by teenagers, but you knew what was going on. Didn't you, Mom?

You knew that I wanted to be student-body president, and how I secretly and deeply regretted that I was never nominated. You knew how difficult it was for me to just barely make the basketball team. I was the little brother of Kent, who was a famous basketball star. I wanted so much to be like him, yet I felt so inferior. You knew I was shy around girls and insecure about my social life. You never said that you knew any of these things, but you did things that showed me that you knew. You must have known, otherwise why did you always do so much to try to build me up? You would tell me I was special. Did you really think that I was special, or that maybe someday I could be?

Did you really think the themes that I wrote for my high-school English class were good? I remember how you'd read every one and tell me that someday I'd be a writer. You never made a big issue about poor spelling, although you were a perfect speller.

You knew what you wanted me to be, didn't you? You always made me feel like you thought I was as perfect as all the other sissies in town. Why didn't you say more about my spelling errors and my other errors in other things? Why did you overlook so many of the problems I had in the here and now, and keep gazing off into the unknown future?

Or was the future really unknown to you, Mom?

If you hadn't been home so much I could have been tougher because then I could have faced up to problems on my own. Take, for instance, the December afternoon so many years ago when I was a high-school senior. I remember that cold afternoon as if it were yesterday. I came home from school and you were there. You were almost always there. You didn't need to be there; I could have made it on my own. But you were there. We had a basketball game that night with Ogden. When I came in and took off my coat, you told me to sit down at our big round table. "I'll cook you a pregame meal." You said it as if I were the one the entire team depended on to be the star.

I was really discouraged that day because I knew I wouldn't get to play at all. You started to fry me a huge pork chop and some potatoes. You kept talking to me about the neighbors and about my married brothers and sisters. I only half listened because I was wishing things could be different for me.

Finally the food was all cooked and you set it before me as if you were serving an all-American. Then you sat down and put your hands together and bowed your head and waited for me to pray. I would have prayed a lot less if you hadn't acted as if nothing good could happen if we didn't ask God for it to happen. I prayed a short prayer. You could sense I was discouraged. You asked me what was wrong. I replied that it didn't make much sense to eat a pregame meal for a bunch of strength and energy when you knew that all you were going to do was sit on the bench. You didn't reply. You just listened. It seems like you liked to talk a lot, but when you and I were alone in the kitchen, as we were so often, you always just wanted to listen.

An hour or so later, when I left to catch the team bus for Ogden, you came over for your kiss on the cheek. You always wanted your kiss on the cheek, didn't you, Mom? It didn't matter to you that tough guys didn't kiss their moms good-bye every time they set foot out of the house. Because of you I got so I couldn't bear to go anywhere without you having your kiss. I'm not sure now if it was you or me who really needed those parting kisses.

The last words that you said that day as I pulled my toboggan hat over my ears were, "You'll do good." I didn't really want to believe you, but I knew I would do well even if I did spend the game on the bench.

Just think, Mom, if you'd been out in the world somewhere on that cold day, you could have given a whole flock of people the courage and encouragement that you gave me. Of course, I liked the way things were in our quiet kitchen, with nobody looking on. Just you and me, Mom. I needed you more than the million others who could have had your influence.

You surely did have a hold on me, Mom. You made it so I never wanted to run away from home. Instead, I always wanted to run home. I'd get homesick just being at school from eight to three. I'd come home, you'd be there—although there were some times when I wondered which came first, me or a Relief Society quilting bee.

You loved to make quilts, didn't you, Mom? You'd put up the long boards in our front room and stretch some cloth on them. Nine or ten ladies would come and you'd all go to work. On those days, when I'd come home from school, you'd shout out a hello. But, much to my despair, I'd have to make my own peanut-butter sandwich.

One afternoon you were in there quilting away and I could hear a lot of unorganized talk. You ladies liked to talk almost as much as Dad and the men down at Chipman's store. Anyway, the general subject that day was the theory that the young people in the town were going to the dogs. They were, according to the talk, worse than any other generation had ever been.

One by one the ladies took turns describing the misbehaviors that were occurring at the high school. I noticed that you were unusually silent throughout this one-sided debate. Finally your voice rose above the regular volume and caused all the others to become silent. I could hear you through the half-closed door. I can still recall every word of your great speech. You said: "I don't know if the kids at the school are doing all that you say they are. All I know is that my son George does not do those things."

You didn't close your talk in the usual "Amen" style, but nonetheless you had just given the most meaningful sermon I had ever heard. Silently, and unknown to you, I pledged to quit doing those things.

Yes, Mom, I have millions of memories. I still feel the gentle hammering of your motherly strokes on my head and on my heart, shaping, ever shaping my every thought and deed.

I guess the truth is that I was a sissy from birth. I tried to hold that kind of behavior back, but your whole goal seemed to be to bring it out. I want so much to be what you want me to be—and once in a while, for a fleeting moment, I am. At those times I am what you, with your gentle influence, have made me.

I am and hope I can forever be a homemade sissy.

A Name That Began with *M*

ELAINE CANNON

We knew a family who had moved along through life on star-spangled wings. There were seven little children all in a tight row, two houses, plentiful holdings, and a place in choice social circles. They were deeply devoted to one another, and as proof of their goal for closeness, mother, father, and every child had a first name that began with the letter *M*. Then, following the birth of a new baby, the mother suddenly, and cruelly it seemed, died.

After a while the father married again. His new wife was young, sophisticated, and successful in glamorous work. She had no children of her own. And her first name did not begin with *M*. People wondered and worried. But she became an energetic friend and counselor to the growing family. One by one the children were carefully guided through peer pressure and homework, and prepared for missions and temple marriage. She added something of herself to their growth, and their lives opened up beyond themselves. She became an other mother, and with the endearing title she earned, her name began with *M* after all!

To My Mother

ELISE RICHINS

I think I loved you the most when I was small, because you took care of me and spent hours doing fun things with me.

Well, I may have loved you more when I was a little older, because you painted my furniture and fixed up my room to make it nice for me.

Or, maybe I loved you the most when I was in Young Women's, because you sewed clothes and costumes for me.

Perhaps I loved you best when I was having growing pains in high school, because you were always there if I needed to talk.

No, I guess I loved you even more when I got married, because you made my dress and worked so hard on my reception to make it lovely and very special.

Now I know—I loved you the very most when my own baby was born, because then I knew how much you loved me.

Who Has Held the Christ Child?

OSCAR W. McCONKIE

Mother was president of the Moab Relief Society. J____ B____ [a nonmember who opposed the Church] had married a Mormon girl. They had several children; now they had a new baby. They were very poor and Mother was going day by day to care for the child and to take them baskets of food, etc. Mother herself was ill, and more than once was hardly able to get home after doing the work at the J____ B____ home.

One day she returned home especially tired and weary. She slept in her chair. She dreamed she was bathing a baby which she discovered was the Christ Child. She thought, Oh, what a great honor to thus serve the very Christ! As she held the baby in her lap, she was all but overcome. She thought, who else has actually held the Christ Child? Unspeakable joy filled her whole being. She was aflame with the glory of the Lord. It seemed that the very marrow in her bones would melt. Her joy was so great it awakened her. As she awoke, these words were spoken to her, "Inasmuch as ye have done it unto one of the least of these my brethren, ye have done it unto me."

A Mother's Faith

"Isn't That an Honor for Me?"

ELAINE CANNON

A friend of mine had enjoyed a rich and lengthy life with a husband who loved her and whom she adored. They'd struggled trying to build a family. Together they'd buried precious loved ones, adopted a child to fill empty heart places. They had coped with financial disaster, awesome professional responsibility, some grave disappointments, and finally with sweet public success.

Out of the details of their life, such closeness came that when death claimed the husband, the woman felt the sun would never shine again. She wondered that people walked the city streets smiling. Then one day she responded to a need and took a volunteer assignment in a local pediatrics hospital. Her job was to register the children being brought there for medical help. All day long she dealt with people with problems, but she was oblivious to them because she wallowed in her own grief. One day there came a mother with a baby so deformed and pitifully stricken that my friend was startled out of her self-centered blindness. The mother of the stricken child was cheerful and friendly and reached into the heart of this widow in a way that swept away bitterness. The baby's mother was a "blessing-counter" and told the widow that she felt especially honored to be given this particularly troubled baby, this unfortunate bit of humanity to care for. "God gave this baby to me because he knew I'd love him well. Isn't that an honor for me?"

A mother taught another mother the lesson of gratitude and confidence before God.

When We Understand the Plan

EDGAR A. GUEST

I reckon when the world we leave
And cease to smile and cease to grieve,
When each of us shall quit the strife
And drop the working tools of life,
Somewhere, somehow, we'll come to find
Just what our Maker had in mind.

Perhaps through clearer eyes than these
We'll read life's hidden mysteries,
And learn the reason for our tears—
Why sometimes came unhappy years,
And why our dearest joys were brief
And bound so closely unto grief.

There is so much beyond our scope,
As blindly on through life we grope,
So much we cannot understand,
However wisely we have planned,
That all who walk this earth about
Are constantly beset by doubt.

No one of us can truly say
Why loved ones must be called away,
Why hearts are hurt, or e'en explain
Why some must suffer years of pain;
Yet some day all of us shall know
The reason why these things are so.

I reckon in the years to come,
When these poor lips of clay are dumb,
And these poor hands have ceased to toil,
Somewhere upon a fairer soil
God shall to all of us make clear
The purpose of our trials here.

For the Love of My Mother

HEBER J. GRANT

There have been many experiences in my life illustrating the benefits that come when we sacrifice our personal ambitions for that which we feel in our heart is our duty. As a boy I had an overwhelming ambition for a university education and a degree from a great school. I had very little hope of obtaining it, having no means and having a widowed mother to look after.

I met President George Q. Cannon, then our delegate to Congress, and he said:

"Heber, would you like to go to the naval academy or West Point?"

I told him I would.

He said: "Which one?"

I said: "The naval academy."

"All right. I will give you the appointment without competitive examination."

For the first time in my life I could not sleep at night; I lay awake nearly all night long rejoicing that the ambition of my life was to be fulfilled. I fell asleep just a little before daylight, and dreamed of what would come to me with an education.

My mother had to wake me, and when I came to breakfast, I said: "Mother, what a marvelous thing it is that I am to have an education as fine as that of any young man in all Utah. I could hardly sleep; I was awake until almost daylight this morning. Isn't it wonderful to think that poor as we are, I am to have this opportunity?"

She said: "Yes, it is." And as I looked into her face, I saw that she had been weeping.

I have heard of people, who, when drowning, had their entire life pass before them in almost a few seconds, and suddenly it flashed through my mind what it would mean to my mother if I were to go out into the world to make my record and be away from her. I was her only child, and I saw myself traveling all over the world in a ship, away from my widowed mother. I laughed and put my arms around her, and kissed her and said:

"Mother, I would not go to Annapolis for all the education and all the glory of all the world. I am going to be a business man and shall enter an office right away and take care of you, and have you quit keeping boarders for a living."

She broke down and wept and said that she had not closed her eyes, but had prayed all night that I would give up my life's ambition so that she would not be left alone.

Now, I have been rewarded for having that spirit in my heart as a boy, notwithstanding my burning ambition for education and for a place among the great names in the world. I sacrificed it all for what? For the love of my mother; and the love of my mother led me to live a life that has brought me to the position that I occupy.

Love God; love and honor your parents; honor your father and your mother that your days may be long; honor your country; live the gospel of Jesus Christ, and God will bless you.

"Who Was Praying for You?"

ANITA R. CANFIELD

It was Christmastime, just a few days before December 25th. A sister from Layton, Utah, welcomed her college children home. Included among the visitors were her recently married son and his bride.

Friday evening after dinner, the young couple told them of their plans to go across the mountain in the morning to a special Christmas fair in Logan, about one hour's drive away. This concerned mother told them to be sure to get up early. A storm was predicted, and she had been over that road enough times in bad weather to know how dangerous it could be. They agreed to leave early and return early.

However, the next morning, everyone slept in until around noon. As her son and daughter-in-law were preparing to leave for the day's outing, this mother looked at the gray skies and felt a little nervous. She asked them to rethink their plans. No, they would be just fine, they said. "Please, Mother, don't worry!" Off they went as she headed for the mall to do last-minute shopping.

Pulling into the parking lot, she saw snow flurries and a sudden sense of fear shook her a little. She bowed her head and said a prayer that her children would be safe and use caution. A feeling of calmness came over her, and she dismissed the anxiety for the moment and headed for the stores.

Returning to her car later, the flurries had now turned into lightly falling snow. She knew this meant much worse weather through and over the mountains. Sliding behind the wheel, her heart pounding frantically, she began to feel tremendous fear once more. Then she remembered her prayer and the calmness that had come.

She began to think how foolish she was feeling. She thought back to her own youth and young married days. Why, there were plenty of times in her life that she had been impulsive and impetuous, thinking nothing of the risks. She remembered often jumping in the car and taking off on adventures. She thought to herself, *and see, nothing happened to me.*

As soon as that thought entered her mind, another one entered her heart, and she heard the words, "Yes, and who do you think was praying for you?"

For the first time in her fifty-some years of living, she realized that as she had been praying for her children, throughout her life there had always been someone praying for her. Since the day she was born someone had continually been praying for her. Not a day in her life had passed without prayers for her. Her parents, her grandparents, her husband, her children, ward members, the bishop, the prophet, perhaps even those on the other side of the veil who had gone before or were yet to come. What remarkable thoughts! What comforting remembrance!

A Mother's Faith

MARION D. HANKS

I heard a noble mother speak once in a stake conference in response to invitation. I'll never forget her. She and her husband and twelve-year-old son lived on a ranch fourteen miles away from the place where they worshipped every Sunday. Saturday night the telephone rang and the twelve-year-old came to his mother with the news that it was Bruce Brown who was asking if he could go with Bruce and another friend and their fathers on a hunting and shooting trip the next morning. He wanted to know what he should tell Bruce.

The mother, as she stood at the pulpit fighting a problem of a lump in the throat, said, "My first impulse was to respond: 'Of course you can't go. Tomorrow is the Sabbath; tomorrow morning is priesthood meeting and Sunday School, and you have obligations.' But I didn't say that." She said she was also tempted to say, "You wait till your father comes in and ask him. He'll have an answer for you." But she didn't say that, either.

Somehow, she found the wisdom and restraint and faith to say: "Son, you're twelve years old. You hold the priesthood of God. You can make up your own mind about that."

He turned away without another word; she went with a prayer in her heart—a prayer with which mothers and fathers, I testify, are familiar: "Lord, Lord, please"—to her own room and knelt down and talked with the Lord. Nothing more was said about the incident.

Father came in, the three of them had their family prayer, went to bed, awakened early the next morning, and prepared for and then went in to priesthood meeting and Sunday School. They parked their pickup truck across the street in a parking lot and were crossing toward the chapel when a truck drove by with guns slung in the window, snowmobiles in the back, and two boys and two laughing men in the front.

The lady at the pulpit then had her hardest moment. She said, "I had hold of the hands of my two men, and as the truck passed the one on the right said, almost inaudibly, 'Gee, I wish . . .' and my heart clutched a moment; then he finished: 'Gee, I wish I could have convinced Bruce that he and Bob ought to be in priesthood meeting this morning.'"

And then we found out the reason for the big lump in the speaker's throat. She said: "We've been particularly grateful we were able to be with him that Sabbath morning, because it was the last Sunday we had him in this world. He was killed in a farm accident that week."

Thank God for a mother's faith, for a mother's wisdom, and a mother's love. There is no more honored place than a mother's, and certainly no more sacred responsibility.

The Consecrated Son

BARBARA B. SMITH

Sarah Melissa Granger was fifteen years old when she went to Kirtland to join the Saints. The records indicate that she was interested in Church doctrines and revelations and that she used to discuss religious matters with her father. Later she attended the School of the Prophets. In her early twenties she married Hiram Kimball. Sarah was a member of the Church, but Hiram was not; he did join the Church later. When their first baby was born, the Nauvoo Temple walls were only about three feet above their foundation. The Saints lacked the money they needed to complete the building. Sarah wanted to make a contribution to the temple project, but she wanted it to be her contribution alone, not her husband's; and even though he was financially well off and could afford to give generously to the Church, contributions from her husband didn't meet her needs as she saw them. She thought a great deal about how she could fulfill her responsibility. Then she had an idea. She had a baby boy just three days old. When her husband came home later that day and came to her bedside to admire the baby, she asked, "What is the boy worth?"

"Oh, I don't know," he said. "He's worth a great deal."

"Is he worth a thousand dollars?" she queried.

"Yes, more than that if he lives and does well."

"Then," she said, "half of him is mine, is it not?"

"Yes, I suppose so," he replied.

"I have something, then, to help with the temple," she said.

"Have you?" questioned her husband.

"Yes, I think I'll turn my share [of the baby] in as tithing," she responded.

"Well, I'll see about that," said her husband.

Soon after that conversation her husband met with the Prophet Joseph. Hiram said, "Sarah proposes to turn over the boy as Church property." He then related their entire discussion to the Prophet.

President Joseph Smith seemed pleased with the joke: "I accept all such donations," was his reply, "and from this day the boy shall stand recorded as Church property." He turned to Willard Richards and directed, "Make a record of this, and you are my witness."

Turning to Hiram, Joseph said, "Major, you now have the privilege of paying $500 and retaining possession, or receiving $500 and giving possession," to which the new father responded, "Will you accept the reserve block of property north of the temple [as payment]?"

"It is just what we want," said the Prophet.

The deed was made out. Later the Prophet said to Sarah, "You have consecrated your firstborn son. For this you are blessed of the Lord. . . . Your name shall be handed down in honorable remembrance from generation to generation."

Mary Fielding Smith and the Power of Prayer

JOSEPH FIELDING SMITH

There had been an arrangement between the authorities of the Church and the leaders of the mob, that the Saints should remain in Nauvoo until the spring of 1846, excepting the poor who would be unable to leave at that time because of their poverty. This agreement was never kept; but it was impossible for all the Saints to evacuate the city as early as the mob desired.

Mary Smith with her family remained in Nauvoo until the summer of 1846. It was only a day or two before the battle of Nauvoo, when, under threats, she hastily loaded her children in a flat boat with such household effects as could be carried, and crossed the Mississippi to a point near Montrose. There under the trees on the bank of the river the family pitched camp that night, and there they experienced the horror of listening to the bombardment of Nauvoo. The oldest son, John, had been privileged to cross the river with a company some time before, but Joseph, then but a boy in his eighth year, heard the roar of guns and was aware of the fact that the remaining Saints were being murdered or driven from their homes.

Here necessity required the mother to leave her little flock camped on the bank of the Mississippi river as she made her way down the river to Keokuk, Iowa, and there negotiated and effected the sale of real estate in Hancock County, Illinois. She received in exchange for this property some wagons, oxen for teams, some horses, cows, etc., and in this manner provided for the transportation of her family across Iowa to Winter Quarters. Although Joseph was not yet eight years of age, he was required to drive one of the ox teams most of the way from Montrose to Winter Quarters. At this place the family sojourned until the spring of 1848, endeavoring in the meantime, by help from friends who were not prepared to continue on the journey, and by constant toil, to gather sufficient teams and necessities to make the journey across the plains. During the winter of 1847–48 Mary Smith made two trips down the Missouri to purchase provisions, and trade for necessities for the family, which numbered in all, about eleven souls. Her son Joseph writing of these trips has said:

"Once I accompanied her, along with my Uncle Joseph Fielding, at which time we went down to St. Joseph, Missouri, and purchased corn and had it ground at Savannah. We also went for the purpose of obtaining provisions and clothing for the family for the coming winter, and for the journey across the plains the following spring. We took two wagons with two yoke of oxen on each. I was almost nine years of age at this time. The weather was unpropitious, the roads were bad, and it rained a great deal during the journey, so that the trip was a very hard, trying and unpleasant one. At St. Joseph we purchased our groceries and dry goods, and at Savannah we laid in our store of flour, meal and corn, bacon and other provisions.

"Returning to Winter Quarters, we camped one evening in an open prairie on the Missouri River bottoms, by the side of a small spring creek, which emptied into the river about three quarters of a mile from us. We were in plain sight of the river, and could apparently see over every foot of the little open prairie where we were camped, to the river on the southwest, to the bluffs on the northwest, and to the timber which skirted the prairie on the right and left. Camping nearby, on the other side of the creek, were some men with a herd of beef cattle, which they were driving to Savannah and St. Joseph for market. We usually unyoked our oxen and turned them loose to feed during our encampments at night, but this time, on account of the proximity of this herd of cattle, fearing that they might get mixed up and driven off with them, we turned our oxen out to feed in their yokes.

"Next morning when we came to look them up, to our great

disappointment our best yoke of oxen was not to be found. Uncle Fielding and I spent all the morning, well nigh until noon, hunting for them, but to no avail. The grass was tall, and in the morning was wet with heavy dew. Tramping through this grass and through the woods and over the bluff, we were soaked to the skin, fatigued, disheartened and almost exhausted.

"In this pitiable plight I was the first to return to our wagons, and as I approached I saw my mother kneeling down in prayer. I halted for a moment and then drew gently near enough to hear her pleading with the Lord not to suffer us to be left in this helpless condition, but to lead us to recover our lost team, that we might continue our travels in safety. When she arose from her knees I was standing nearby. The first expression I caught upon her precious face was a lovely smile, which discouraged as I was, gave me renewed hope and an assurance I had not felt before.

"A few moments later Uncle Joseph Fielding came to the camp, wet with the dews, faint, fatigued and thoroughly disheartened. His first words were: 'Well, Mary, the cattle are gone!' Mother replied in a voice which fairly rang with cheerfulness, 'Never mind; your breakfast has been waiting for hours, and now, while you and Joseph are eating, I will just take a walk out and see if I can find the cattle.' My uncle held up his hands in blank astonishment, and if the Missouri River had suddenly turned to run up stream, neither of us could have been much more surprised. 'Why, Mary,' he exclaimed, 'what do you mean? We have been all over this country, all through the timber and through the herd of cattle, and our oxen are gone—they are not to be found. I believe they have been driven off, and it is useless for you to attempt to do such a thing as to hunt for them.'

" 'Never mind me,' said mother, 'get your breakfast and I will see,' and she started towards the river, following down spring creek. Before she was out of speaking distance the man in charge of the herd of beef cattle rode up from the opposite side of the creek and called out: 'Madam, I saw your oxen over in that direction this morning about daybreak,' pointing in the opposite direction from that in which mother was going. We heard plainly what he said, but mother went right on, and did not even turn her head to look at him. A moment later the man rode off rapidly toward his herd, which had been gathered in the opening near the edge of the woods, and they were soon under full drive for the road leading toward Savannah, and soon disappeared from view.

"My mother continued straight down the little stream of water, until she stood almost on the bank of the river, and then she beckoned to us. I was watching her every moment and was determined that she should not get out of my sight. Instantly we rose from the 'mess-chest,' on which our breakfast had been spread, and started toward her, and like John, who outran the other disciple to the sepulchre, I outran my uncle and came first to the spot where my mother stood.

"There I saw our oxen fastened to a clump of willows growing in the bottom of a deep gulch which had been washed out of the sandy bank of the river by the little spring creek, perfectly concealed from view. We were not long in releasing them from bondage and getting back to our camp, where the other cattle had been fastened to the wagon wheels all the morning, and we were soon on our way home rejoicing. The **worthy** herdsmen had suddenly departed when they saw mother would not heed them; I hope they went in search of estray honesty, which I trust they found."

$\mathscr{A}$ Bright Red Shawl

CAMILLA WOODBURY JUDD

In May, 1856, [Robert and Ann Hartley Parker] with their four children, Max, 12; Martha Alice, 10; Arthur, 5; and Ada, one year old, left England by sailing vessel to join the Saints in Utah. . . . They went by rail to Iowa City where they continued their journey by handcart. All had their share of the work. Robert and Ann pulled the heavily loaded cart, Maxie pushed and Martha Alice followed with the younger children, taking care of little brother Arthur.

. . . Robert Parker was stricken with fever that was sweeping the company and [had to be] placed in one of the wagons. Martha Alice had to leave her little brother to the care of the other children while she lent her child-strength to the heavy cart.

One day, while going through the timberlands of Nebraska, Arthur became feverish and ill and, unnoticed by the other children, sat down to rest beside the trail. He was soon fast asleep. In the afternoon a sudden storm came up and the company hurried to make camp. Finding that Arthur was not with the children, they hurriedly organized a posse and went back to search for him. They returned with grim faces after two days' searching. The captain ordered the company to move on. Ann pleaded with him, but he set his jaw hard—the food was giving out and not another day could be lost.

Ann Parker pinned a bright shawl about the thin shoulders of her husband and sent him back alone on the trail to search again for their child. If he found him dead he was to wrap him in the shawl; if alive, the shawl would be a flag to signal her. Ann and her children took up their load and struggled on with the company, while Robert retraced the miles of forest trail, calling, and searching and praying for his helpless little son. At last he reached a mail and trading station where he learned that his child had been found and cared for by a woodsman and his wife. He had been ill from exposure and fright. [But] God had heard the prayers of his people.

Out on the trail each night Ann and her children kept watch, and when, on the third night, the rays of the setting sun caught the glimmer of a bright red shawl, the brave little mother sank in a pitiful heap in the sand. Completely exhausted, Ann slept for the first time in six long days and nights. God indeed was kind and merciful, and in the gladness of their hearts the Saints sang, "All Is Well."

Act of Faith

MARILYNNE TODD LINFORD

My friend Karen and her husband tried every known scientific and medical method to have children, costing thousands of dollars and a roller coaster of emotions. They prayed, fasted, went to the temple often—and still no baby. Some years ago they contacted LDS Social Services and were placed on an adoption waiting list.

One day Karen answered the phone at work to hear the good news that they had been chosen as adoptive parents. The baby was due in a week. There was joy and rejoicing. Karen gave notice at her work. She began to turn the empty bedroom into a nursery—something she had never been willing to do before. She basked in this incredible, blessed turn of events.

The week passed without word on the status of their baby. Another few days went painfully by. They sensed something had gone wrong. The work on the nursery stopped. Then the phone call came explaining that the baby had been born on its due date and the birth mother had decided to keep it. Devastation is too gentle a word to describe the feelings of Karen and her husband. The tears, the questions, the grieving were felt by everyone who knew and loved this couple. One friend, trying to make her feel better, said, "Karen, you've done everything possible. You just have to get on with life and keep the faith."

That simple statement gave birth to a frightening idea. Karen asked herself, what faith could she keep? She had thought the thought before, but she could almost feel what it would be like to pass an empty nursery day after day, week after week, year after year, perhaps for a lifetime. She asked her husband what he thought about the idea of finishing the nursery; it would be an act of faith, she reasoned. They decided to do it. Every night after work they painted, wallpapered, put up a border, made matching ruffly curtains, and recarpeted. They purchased a crib. They kept finding little projects to make this nursery unique. When the nursery was finished, the weight of what they had created caused Karen flashes of fear. She made herself a sign—a quote from Elder Neal A. Maxwell—"Go forward with faith."

After about two weeks, the adoption agency called again wanting to know if they were still interested in that baby. "The same baby?" Karen asked incredulously. "Yes, the birth mother has tried and just can't do it. All the papers are signed. The baby is here. Can you come pick her up?" Karen's thoughts raced: *Right now? Come? It's a girl! She is ours!!*

Congratulations, Karen, for going forward in love and faith.

It Was His Duty

ANITA R. CANFIELD

One of my sons had planned all of his life to go on a mission. When he turned eighteen and a half his plans changed. In fact, he grew further and further away from not only a mission but also his spirituality.

As his nineteenth birthday approached, his dad and I tried to open a discussion with him about his mission. He didn't want to talk about it. So we took him on a three-day camping trip, though personally I would rather slam my hand in a car door than go camping! Because he knew this about his mother, he realized how much we wanted to understand his heart and his thoughts. During that trip he expressed some concerns over his future, concerns over the unknowns, concerns that his testimony was truly his own. The talks drew us all closer, but he still did not want to go on a mission.

He turned nineteen on a Sunday. That Saturday evening before his birthday I went into his room to say good night and tried one more time to say words that would inspire him to reconsider.

Instead, he became more upset with me and told me he felt that I was trying too hard to persuade him to go. He let me know he felt I was wrong to discuss this with him and that my thoughts were no longer welcome. He said, "I don't think I *want* to go. I think if you go on a mission you ought to have the *desire* to go. It has to be your desire and you have to think it will be good for you to go."

I left his room feeling that I had made the situation worse, really sorry I had said anything more. As I prayed later, I asked for inspiration. What could I do? What should I do? Was there something that would reach him? Should I do nothing more?

As I woke up the next morning a clear and distinct thought came immediately into my mind. I searched through some Church videotapes until I found the message that had come into my mind. I went in his room and woke him up to say happy birthday; then I invited him downstairs in front of the television.

I put in the VCR a video entitled *Family Home Evening,* and told him I was only going to play the first one minute and then turn it off.

The introductory music stopped, and there stood President Ezra Taft Benson addressing the congregation assembled in the Tabernacle in Salt Lake City. In that brief segment he declared that it was the duty of every young man to serve a full-time mission. I turned the tape off as promised, turned to my son, and told him that it would be wonderful if he had the desire to go; that it would be even better if he really wanted to go; but that neither of those things mattered. As spoken from the mouth of a prophet, it was his *duty* to go. And then I promised him that if he would just go out of duty, the desire would come and he would be blessed beyond anything he could ever do on his own. He would become the man he was meant to be.

He didn't seem very happy all day. He was unusually quiet. But that evening, that Sunday evening on his nineteenth birthday, dressed in a shirt and tie, with scriptures in hand, he came downstairs to tell us he was on his way to see the bishop.

During the next months of preparation the Holy Ghost came to help my son. He gave him a witness that the preparation was God's work and that true principles were involved. He helped him fill his heart with a sincere and enthusiastic desire to go. A few months later, on a Wednesday afternoon, we took him to the Missionary Training Center in Provo, Utah, to commence his path of duty.

You can imagine the joy we felt over the months that followed as we read of his tremendous love for his mission and for the people, especially for the people. He wrote of his sacrifices and how it was a blessing to him to have this mission and those sacrifices. He wrote of the sorrow at seeing those whom he served reject the gospel and of his utter joy at seeing others accept it. He wrote profound words of his love of the Savior and his deepened testimony of the Prophet Joseph Smith and the Book of Mormon. He wrote very emotionally of his gratitude for being raised in the gospel and knowing the truth. He was called to serve as district leader, then zone leader, and finally assistant to the mission president. He grew in leadership talent, spirituality, faith, and wisdom.

And when it was time for him to leave his missionary service he had mixed emotions about coming home.

I think back on the words of President Benson, and I know there is safety in simply living the life of a Latter-day Saint and doing one's duty to the Lord.

An Unfinished Woman

JAROLDEEN ASPLUND EDWARDS

Here am I, Lord,
The dishes barely done and night long since fallen,
The children would not go to bed
And would not go and
Would not go—
And now they are gone.
Gone to places of their own with children of their own
Who will not go to bed and will not go . . .
And I have taught them what I could and
They have learned the things they would
And now they've gone their way alone to learn the rest
Most on their own.

And I remain, not half spent.
And I remain, not yet content,
So much to do, so much to learn,
So much to feel, so much to yearn.
My past mistakes make stepping-stones,
Not millstones great around my neck but
Stones to guide my searching feet—
And I must search; I'm incomplete.

I watch my years go tumbling by
And I must use them better, I
Have yet so much to learn and do
Before I can return to You.

The hour is late. The night comes on,
My celestial self I would become.
Ah! What wisdom thou gavest to mortal life—

I,
As sister, mother, daughter, wife—
In earthly roles have seen Thy face.
In my womanly life Thy heavenly place
Is taught through humble tasks and pain.
So, if royal robes I would obtain,
To wear as all Thy glories burst—
I'll need to do the laundry first.

"*L*eave It Alone"

MARILYNNE TODD LINFORD

A friend told me of a day she received two phone calls—one from the high school counselor and one from the seminary teacher. Both calls told her the same thing—that her son had been sluffing school. She felt betrayed. She had trusted this child.

He had stopped home briefly after school that day and then left. At 10:30 P.M. she had no idea where he was. He was not supposed to go out on school nights. Her anger began to increase. By 10:45 she had a plan. She would be waiting for him in the living room when he came home. By 11:00 she was nearly distraught. She had mentally created a list of unexplained actions that she wanted answers for. Being grounded for the rest of his life seemed a fitting punishment. At 11:15 she began to think he was dead someplace. At 11:30 she decided to pray to see if her planned assault on him when (or if) he came home was right. As soon as she knelt, even as she was saying the first words, the Spirit hinted to her, *Leave it alone.* She answered back, *How can I leave it alone? He's been sluffing school. I have no idea where he's been for hours.* The thought came again, *Go to bed and leave it alone.*

She turned to go to her room, when she heard his car. She wanted to be obedient to the prompting, so she dove into bed with her clothes on. She waited. Soon there was a knock at the bedroom door. "Mom, I'm sorry I'm so late. I know you've been worried. May I come in and talk to you?" She could tell there was a conciliatory sound in his voice. She invited him in. She listened. He opened up. He explained where he had been and what changes he knew were necessary in his life.

How grateful she was for the prompting and for her obedience!

A Mother's Influence

♪inging Lessons

MAX AND BETTE MOLGARD

Max Jr. was in tenth grade when he came home from school and announced to his mother, Bette, that he was going to try out for a part in the school musical. Tryouts were just three short days away, and full of the optimism he had always possessed, he queried, "Mom, will you teach me how to sing?"

Max had sat with the deacons since his voice had changed, and Bette realized that she hadn't heard Max sing for years. His childhood voice had certainly been nothing to brag about. But, she reasoned, surely the years had brought improvement. She thought that people were either born with a pretty voice or not, so she would know if he could sing the minute she played a song on the piano and had him follow along.

That idea failed miserably. There was never a match of Max's voice to the notes his mother played on the piano. In short, his voice was among the top contenders for the worst voice she had ever heard. But how could she break this fact to Max?

She looked into his expectant eyes and decided to try a new strategy. She would play just one note on the piano and have him match it with his voice. After fifteen minutes of trying, the match had not been made. Her stomach was in knots as she thought about the humiliation they would feel if they shared his voice with others.

Not about to be totally discouraged, she decided that he could sing a note and she would match it with the piano. Once a match was made, she went down the scale and found that he had taken enough music lessons on his trumpet to know what the steps and half steps sounded like. In this time-consuming manner, they would arrive at the first note of the chosen song, and he could proceed from there with semi-satisfactory results. Bette knew that they wouldn't be totally humiliated at tryouts if she prayed mightily that he could find the first note.

The day of tryouts, Max combined his lack of musical skills with the fact that he was nervous and sang his heart out as he missed every note they had practiced. Bette thought to herself that if she had been him, that would have been the last time anyone heard her sing in public. But Max was not discouraged. "I think I'd better take voice lessons if I ever want to be a lead in a school musical," he said.

Bette rolled her eyes and wondered where she would ever find a teacher who would have the patience to work with someone who would never be able to learn to sing.

She found that teacher in a woman named Jean Poyer. Jean had an amazing way of knowing where the sound needed to come from and how to progress step by step until her students could reach their full potential. Bette knew that Max's full potential wouldn't be wonderful, but she couldn't discourage him from trying. He started lessons the following week.

Months passed. Max worked diligently on his lessons, and Jean seemed to be pleased. Bette wrote out the monthly checks for the voice lessons and thought of how many other things the family could have spent that money on. It seemed a bit of a waste, but she was willing to appease Max, at least for a little while. In the meantime, she encouraged him to practice back in his bedroom behind a closed door. She didn't think her musical ear could handle too much up-close practice time.

For Mother's Day that year, Max wrote a song for his mom. He asked her to go for a ride in the truck, and there in the privacy of the cab he sang his heart out. With tears streaming down her cheeks, Bette was surprised at how much Max's voice had improved. The notes were a little flat here and there, but it was tolerable. And the music he had written coupled with the words of his heart remain as a memory that will be treasured always.

Max joined a singing group and practiced weekly for their

spiritual sacrament meeting presentations. Bette went to watch and could hear an improvement with each passing week. He tried out for the school musical his junior year and got a part in the chorus.

With continued effort, the miracle unfolded. By the time try-outs came around for the annual musical during his senior year, Max was fully prepared. As he completed his solo for the tryouts, his drama coach kiddingly asked where he had hidden the tape recorder. Bette accompanied his tryout and left the stage with a lump in her throat, bursting with pride.

Max was not given the lead in the school musical that year. But he had a part that required a vocal solo and worked hard during rehearsals. *The Unsinkable Molly Brown* was the musical chosen that year. Then just ten days before opening night, the male lead decided that he couldn't pull it off. Even though his voice was full and beautiful, his inexperience with acting left him uncomfortable with the part of Johnny Brown. That afternoon, Bette returned home to find a note: "Dear Mom and Dad," it said, "I won't be home until late tonight, and you probably won't see me much for the next ten days. I'm Johnny Brown!"

On opening night, some people might have judged that although Max's acting ability was marvelous and his voice was nice, it wasn't the most beautiful voice they had ever heard in a high school musical. But those who knew what Max's leading role had entailed could only clap louder during the standing ovation on closing night.

$\mathcal{T}$he Educated Parent

KATHLEEN "CASEY" NULL

In our society we feel it is of utmost importance to prepare ourselves well for certain careers. A lawyer needs law school; a doctor, medical school. But what kind of education does a parent require?

College was a smorgasbord to me. "Let's see," I'd say, poring over class schedules and catalogs, "I'll take some of that, and some of this—and oh, look at that!"

I ended up with two majors and a minor that was almost a major. And I took a broad sampling from several other fields as well. It took me fifteen years to graduate with a B.A., and at that time I already had several graduate-level credits accumulated as an undergraduate. I've been at the graduate level for five years now.

I love learning. It's just that simple. And that complicated. But what, you might have asked me had you known me, were my career goals?

If I had had the insight then that I do now (insight that I didn't get within the walls of any classroom), I would have told you the following:

Since I will be raising four highly energetic, creative, and curious children while juggling Church callings and work in creative fields, I will need

• An extensive background in psychology so that I will have the tools to deal with children who will predictably do the unpredictable. I will need to know how to motivate children to do mundane things while their heads are in the clouds. And I will need to understand, as nearly as possible, what is in their heads so that I don't lose my own sanity. And I will need to understand why I feel the way I do when I am suffering from postpartum depression and exhaustion, trying to nurse a fussy newborn, and I hear the other children playing on the roof.

• A background in math and economics so that I will be able to figure out how to feed a meal to six people for $2.35, buy a back-to-school wardrobe for four for $175, and compute tithing and IOUs for four allowances.

• A background in dietetics so that the $2.35 meal for six is also nutritious.

• A background in health so that I will be capable of administering appropriate first aid three times a week, answering countless questions about "Why is that lady sticking out so far in her stomach?" and offering scientific explanations about why the bedroom must be cleaner than that.

• A background in education so that I can attend parent-teacher conferences without an interpreter, supervise homework assignments, know how to find out how many miles it is to Jupiter, and teach my children (i.e., answer their questions).

• A background in sociology and social psychology so that I can understand (if not condone) my teenager's actions.

• A background in literature and music so that I can tell entertaining bedtime stories and have a repertoire of sing-alongs for long car trips.

• A background in theology so that even on the most trying days I can comfort myself with thoughts of more exalted days.

In the challenges of family life I can say with a certainty that I have found myself relying upon every resource I possess. My education has been truly useful.

Parenthood is the most challenging career there is. It requires wholehearted immersion. It's a learn-on-the-job situation. It's not for the faint-of-heart. But then, the growth and learning that result are invaluable by-products.

The Record of Her Labors

ARDETH G. KAPP

As my mother and I sat quietly listening to the many praises expressed in beautiful music and tender words, I glanced at her graying hair and her thin hands folded together in her lap, a white handkerchief bordered with lace tucked between her fingers.

It was Mother's Day, and the program, while it had followed the traditional pattern, seemed especially inspiring this year. The personal examples given as testimonies of true motherhood were expressed by persons of all ages. We were taught by the Spirit as each speaker expressed tender feelings of the heart. I felt a reverence for life itself, and an increased awareness of my debt of gratitude to the mother sitting beside me—she who, over the years, had experienced many challenges, blessings, and rewards, and some heartaches, each leaving in its wake evidence of the aging process so much a part of this mortal life. Just a few short years ago Mother was a child herself, and then a wife and mother, and now a grandmother. And the wheel turns ever so quickly.

With trembling hands she now graciously accepted a small pot of pink begonias, as did each mother up and down the rows. As she sat holding this small token of appreciation, I heard again in my mind the comment she had made when we entered the chapel. Half to herself, yet audible to me, she had said, "You know, I don't like Mother's Day. It always reminds me of the things I could have done and didn't." Then she added, with a serious note, "I hear about the ideal mother and wonder how my children have done so well."

While the little plants were presented to each mother, I wondered about the praises so generously given. Were they as readily accepted? Or were some held in reserve in the minds of many mothers for those who they thought were more deserving?

The question of eligibility for such honors might be raised as a mother thinks back on those times of stress when her own children emphatically declare that someone else's mother is more understanding, more trusting, and certainly more patient, even though she knows that those very times might be evidences of greater love that qualify her for the honor. And so it is that mothers of all ages may see themselves falling short of that ideal which they would hope might one day be within their reach, little realizing that at that very moment they stand on the threshold of greatness. The self-recorded ledger, which might otherwise reveal an excess of assets, may appear lacking because the recording is incomplete. It is in the heart and soul of the child, and not the ledger kept by the mother, that the record of her labors is more accurately recorded, just as the epistles of Christ were "written not with ink, but with the Spirit of the living God; not in tables of stone, but in fleshy tables of the heart." (2 Corinthians 3:3.)

Years ago the president of a large company gave the following account: "I remember, when I was very young, a mother with three children who had very little in the way of worldly goods; on birthdays and other special days the most she could do was to give her children a small toy made with her own hands. However, she always did something else which in my mind was worth more than the most expensive toy ever made. On a child's birthday she would call him into the bedroom, sit him down in a chair, and then kneel down to pray. In her prayer, she would thank her God for blessing her with this child, and she would enumerate the pleasures that the child had given her, and pray for his continued health and happiness. . . . I can only express my personal opinion, but I do believe that there are many children today who have very expensive toys, but who would trade them all for such an experience." (*Fedco Reporter,* June 1957, p. 25.)

I wonder if the magnitude of that experience went unrecorded except in the life of the child.

And what of the mother whose little second grader, in the midst of snickering from his classmates, stood tall and responded to the teacher's inquiry as to who might like to be a neighbor to cross old Mr. Black in the story they had just heard. The boy's mother was unaware of her teaching recorded in the heart of her child, a teaching that rippled out to everyone in the class, as her son looked first at the teacher, then at the children, and said with conviction, "I wish Mr. Black was my neighbor, because if he was my neighbor, my mom would bake a pie for me to take to him. Then he wouldn't be that way anymore." Another child responded, "I wish I'd said that." And a mother's labors were recorded in the "fleshy tables of the heart" of her child and others.

$\mathcal{S}$he Taught Me to Pray

GEORGE ALBERT SMITH

We are in the habit of erecting monuments to men. I want to tell you . . . the most enduring monuments in this world have been erected in the home by women. I feel to say . . . that I love my father—no man could love his father more—but when I think of the influence of my mother when I was a little tad I am moved to reverence and tears. When my father was away in the mission field, I remember as though it were yesterday, she took me by the hand and we walked up a flight of stairs to the second story. There I knelt before her and held her hand as she taught me to pray. Thank God for those mothers who have in their hearts the spirit of the gospel and a desire to bless. I could repeat that prayer now and it is a great many years since I learned it. It gave me an assurance that I had a Heavenly Father, and let me know that he heard and answered prayer.

When I was older we still lived in a two-story frame house and when the wind blew hard it would rock as if it would topple over. Sometimes I would be too frightened to go to sleep. My bed was in a little room by itself, and many a night I have climbed out and got down on my knees and asked my Father in Heaven to take care of the house, preserve it that it would not break in pieces, and I have got back into my little bed just as sure that I would be safeguarded from evil as if I held my Father's hand. What a power our Heavenly Father has bestowed upon you mothers.

The Reading Mother

STRICKLAND GILLILAN

I had a Mother who read to me
Sagas of pirates who scoured the sea,
Cutlasses clenched in their yellow teeth,
"Blackbirds" stowed in the hold beneath.

I had a Mother who read me lays
Of ancient and gallant and golden days;
Stories of Marmion and Ivanhoe,
Which every boy has a right to know.

I had a Mother who read me tales
Of Gêlert the hound of the hills of Wales,
True to his trust till his tragic death,
Faithfulness blent with his final breath.

I had a Mother who read me the things
That wholesome life to the boy heart brings—
Stories that stir with an upward touch,
Oh, that each mother of boys were such!

You may have tangible wealth untold;
Caskets of jewels and coffers of gold.
Richer than I you can never be—
I had a Mother who read to me.

$\mathcal{A}$ndy's Talk

MICHAELENE P. GRASSLI

My cousin's five-year-old son, Andy, was assigned to give a talk in Primary. His mother said, "Let's decide what you're going to say."

"Oh, it's all right," he responded. "I know what I'm going to say."

Mothers just aren't usually too comfortable with that, so in a day or two she tried again. He reassured her that he knew what he was going to say. So on Saturday his mother said, "Andrew, let's pretend you're at Primary and practice what you're going to say so you won't be nervous when it's your turn."

With a sigh he conceded. To please his mother he would practice. He said, as he held up his own Book of Mormon, "In our family, we read the Book of Mormon together every day. We take turns reading. When it's my turn, since I can't read yet, my daddy reads for me and then I tell what it's about.

"I've learned a lot reading the Book of Mormon. Nephi was a good example. I hope I can be a good example like Nephi.

"I think it's a good thing to read the Book of Mormon. Children should read it. We can all read the Book of Mormon."

Andy's mother knew then that he would be all right giving his talk.

Always

CAROLYN SESSIONS ALLEN

Once a mother, always a mother."

As my children have matured, I've gained new insight into the meaning of this phrase. Mothering spans the generations. I'm wondering just how far into the eternities a mother's influence will continue.

You know mothering goes on forever when:

—Your grandmother still tells your mother how to cook the macaroni.

—Your mother complains that your hair is getting too gray.

—Your married daughter calls long-distance to tell you that her kitty has run away.

—You still wait up for a twenty-three-year-old returned missionary.

—You find another mother on the fourth grade field trip who has more grandchildren than you.

—The conversation with a group of friends centers on concern for not-yet-married sons.

—You find yourself fascinated, once more, with "Sesame Street" as you watch it with a grandchild.

—You keep asking your working married daughter when her husband is going to get a job.

—You keep asking your home-for-the-summer son when he's going to get a job.

—You attend Girls Camp with your youngest daughter and find that some of her contemporaries are grandchildren of some of your contemporaries.

—Your children, too old for allowances, still need occasional financial backing.

—You worry about your adult children not taking life seriously enough.

—You worry about your married children taking life too seriously.

"Mom Says I Shouldn't Go"

GEORGE D. DURRANT

I recall that once, when I was a young man, several of my friends said they had a trip planned to Las Vegas and asked if I could go with them. I think I was a senior in high school at the time. You know, that's about the age when you start thinking you can make your own decisions. I told Mom that I was going to Las Vegas with my buddies. She calmly asked me what we were going down for, how long we would be gone, and so on. I gave her what I thought were good answers. I was polite and kind and considerate.

She didn't say much more about it, and finally it came time for us to go. I had a little bag packed; and as I walked out toward the car my mother followed me out. "George," she said, "come back just a minute, will you?"

I said, "Sure, Mom," and stepped back into the house.

"George," she said, "don't go."

"Gee, Mom," I protested, "they're waiting for me. I promised to go. I want to go. It'll be a good little vacation for me, and I've got the money to go."

"George, don't go," she repeated.

"But why, Mom?" I asked.

"I don't know why," she replied, "but please don't go."

"Mom, I've got to go," I insisted.

Yet again she said, "Don't go."

Now a strange feeling began to come over me. "Mom, why?" I asked again.

This time she said, "I just know you shouldn't go."

The feeling had now become so overwhelming that I just walked out of the house and said to my friends, "I can't go."

They began to get upset. "Why not?" they asked.

I replied, "Because my mom says I shouldn't go."

Of course, they tried to persuade me, then finally to taunt me into going. "Ah, come on. What are you, some kind of a mama's boy?"

I simply said, "No, I'm not a mama's boy, but she said I shouldn't go and I'm not going."

They finally gave up on me and drove away in some degree of disgust.

Two days later I learned that my friends' car had turned over several times as they were traveling down the highway late at night and that all four of those fellows had been thrown out. Not one of them had been seriously injured; one was knocked unconscious for a time, but he was revived and he had no aftereffects. The police officer said it was a miracle someone hadn't been killed. I've always wondered what would have happened if there had been five fellows in that car. I wonder if five would have been as lucky as four. I guess I'll never know. But I do know that my mom knew I shouldn't go; and I know now, as I knew then, that she was right.

A Little Parable for Mothers

TEMPLE BAILEY

The Young Mother set her foot on the path of life.

"Is the way long?" she asked.

And her Guide said: "Yes. And the way is hard. And you will be old before you reach the end of it. But the end will be better than the beginning."

But the Young Mother was happy, and she would not believe that anything could be better than these years. So she played with her children and gathered flowers for them along the way, and bathed with them in the clear streams; and the sun shone on them, and life was good, and the young Mother cried, "Nothing will ever be lovelier than this."

Then came night, and storm, and the path was dark, and the children shook with fear and cold, and the Mother drew them close and covered them with her mantle, and the children said, "Oh, Mother, we are not afraid, for you are near, and no harm can come," and the Mother said, "This is better than the brightness of day, for I have taught my children courage."

And the morning came and there was a hill ahead, and the children climbed and grew weary, but at all times she said to the children, "A little patience, and we are there." So the children climbed and grew weary, and the Mother was weary, but at all times she said to the children, "A little patience, and we are there." So the children climbed, and when they reached the top, they said, "We could not have done it without you, Mother." And the Mother, when she lay down that night, looked up at the stars, and said: "This is a better day than the last, for my children have learned fortitude in the face of hardness. Yesterday I gave them courage. Today I have given them strength."

And the next day came strange clouds which darkened the earth—clouds of war and hate and evil, and the children groped and stumbled, and the Mother said: "Look up. Lift your eyes to the Light." And the children looked and saw above the clouds an Everlasting Glory, and it guided them and brought them beyond the darkness. And that night the Mother said, "This is the best day of all, for I have shown my children God."

And the days went on, and the weeks and the months and the years, and the Mother grew old, and she was little and bent. But her children were tall and strong, and walked with courage. And when the way was hard, they helped their Mother; and when the way was rough, they lifted her, for she was light as a feather; and at last they came to a hill, and beyond the hill they could see a shining road and golden gates flung wide.

And the Mother said: "I have reached the end of my journey. And now I know that the end is better than the beginning, for my children can walk alone, and their children after them."

And the children said, "You will always walk with us, Mother, even when you have gone through the gates."

And they stood and watched her as she went on alone, and the gates closed after her. And they said: "We cannot see her, but she is with us still. A Mother like ours is more than a memory. She is a Living Presence."

Teaching Moments

"You're Lucky Too"

JOYCE ERICKSON

Editor's Note: Of the six children born to Bruce and Joyce Erickson, three had a serious disability that left them totally dependent on their parents. The following story is about one of those disabled children, the Ericksons' only son, Mark.

Mark had just arrived home from school—a time that is usually happy for him—and I could tell when I saw him coming down on the bus wheelchair lift that he was ready to cry. Sure enough, as soon as I got him into the living room the tears came quickly and freely. I immediately took him out of his wheelchair, held him close, and let him cry for a couple of minutes.

Finally I interrupted his crying and said, "You really feel bad, Mark. Did something happen at school today?"

"Yes," he said as he began to cry hard again.

I said, "Mark, I can't understand you while you're crying. You'll have to quit if you want me to understand you."

He said, "Okay," and finally quit crying. Then he said, "Mom, the boys at school are so lucky."

"Why do you think they're lucky, Mark?"

"They can run, play football. They can run fast and run races." With those words, he started to cry once again. My heart ached for him. I held him close and let him cry while I tried to think of something to say.

Without knowing beforehand exactly what I would say, I began, "Mark, you think the boys at school are really lucky, don't you?"

"Yes," he said.

"Well," I said, "they are lucky, Mark. But do you know something? Everyone is lucky in some way. Did you know that?"

"No," he said.

"Well, they are."

Then, without ever having thought about it before, I held up my left hand, and, pointing to each finger as I spoke, I said, "Mark, your friends are lucky because they can run, play football, ride bikes, play computer games, write—"

"And draw," Mark said.

"Yes, and draw. But do you know what, Mark? You're lucky too." I held up my right hand. "You're lucky because you got to go into the BYU locker room and meet the BYU football players, and you're lucky because you got to go into the BYU locker room and meet the basketball players; you got to sing with the Tabernacle Choir and meet Brother Ottley—"

"And go on the USS *Nimitz,*" Mark said.

"Yes, and do you know how else you're lucky, Mark?"

"No," he said.

"You're lucky because *everyone* likes you. I don't know of anyone who doesn't like you. Did you know that one of your friends once said to me, 'Mark is so lucky. I wish I had as many friends as Mark has.' And when you were running for governor of the fourth grade, a girl who was running against you said, 'It really isn't fair. Everyone knows Mark, and everyone likes him.' Did you know that?"

"No," he said again as his whole countenance brightened.

"And do you know how else you're lucky, Mark? You're lucky because Satan can't tempt you. He can tempt your friends to disobey their parents, to steal, to cheat, to be mean to other people—but he can't tempt you to do any of those things. Did you know that, Mark?"

"Yes," he said in a happy tone.

"Everyone's just lucky in different ways. Your friends are lucky in these ways," I said as I held up my left hand, "and you're lucky in these ways," I said, holding up my right hand.

Mark readily agreed, but for some reason I continued one step further. I held up both hands and asked, "Mark, if you had a choice, which hand would you choose? Would you choose to be lucky like your friends?" I held up my left hand. "Or would you choose to be lucky like you are now?" I held up my right hand.

Without hesitating, Mark looked directly at my right hand and said, "I choose that hand."

"Well, Mark," I said, "that's the one I think you chose before you were born, when you lived with Heavenly Father."

"Yeah, I know," Mark replied happily.

I was so thankful that the Spirit had inspired me with the right words to say, because finally Mark was comforted. He felt peace because he understood and was touched by the Spirit, and I felt peace because I was able to comfort and console him through the help of the "still small voice."

"Good Breathing, Son!"

GLENN I. LATHAM

Some years ago, while I was giving a talk to parents in Salt Lake City at the Governor's Conference on Families, a mother raised her hand and asked, "What am I to do with my 17-year-old son? I can't think of anything good about him to acknowledge. He looks bad, he smells bad, he is bad. I haven't even seen him for several days. What am I supposed to do when he comes home?"

I answered, "When he comes home, lift your head high, square your shoulders, smile, look him right in the eye, and say, 'Good breathing, Son.' " She looked at me as though I were kidding and asked, "What did you say?"

I repeated what I had told her and added, "Let him know you're glad he's home safe and sound and that you've been concerned about him." I also assured her that I was dead serious about what I had advised her to do.

A few days later in my office at Utah State University, I got a phone call. It was that mother. She excitedly told me what had happened. It went something like this: "My son came home last night. He looked bad, he smelled bad, and I'm sure he had been bad. Fighting off the urge to be negative, I stood tall, smiled, looked him right in the eye, and said, 'Good breathing, Son!' He looked at me as though he hadn't understood what I said, and asked, 'What did you say, Mother?' I answered, 'I'm glad you're still breathing, Son. And I'm glad you're home safe and sound. I've been worried about you!'

"We just stood there looking at each other. Then he smiled back, walked over to me, put his arms around me, kissed my cheek, and told me he loved me."

The Bicycle Lesson

ARDETH G. KAPP

My sister Shirley, with her family of young children, described the routine schedule of her day as one crisis after another in constant regularity. One problem in this family was the habit of leaving bicycles in the driveway. According to a decision made in family council, those who left bicycles in the driveway were subject to punishment; they were to be grounded for a week.

Glancing out the kitchen window one day, Shirley saw the familiar sight—two bicycles in the driveway. It was this teaching moment that loomed more important than any other, if her children were to learn the language of the Lord through the scriptures and find the solutions to childhood problems in gospel principles.

Calling her son Lincoln to her side, she explained, "Lincoln, Jennifer has left her bike in the driveway. What do you think we should do? Should we ground her or give her another chance?" Without remembering his own negligence, he spoke in defense of his younger sister. "Oh, Mom, give her another chance. She just forgot. Give her one more chance and I'll help her remember."

Dismissing Lincoln, she then called Jennifer to her side. "Jennifer," she said, "Lincoln has left his bicycle in the driveway. What do you think we should do? Should we ground him or give him another chance?" Jenny, free-spirited and always quick to respond, did not hesitate. "Ground him," she said. "That was the decision. Ground him."

A different answer might have required less time, but the time for this lesson was now. Calling both children to her side, Shirley said, "Lincoln, if you will take your bicycle out of the driveway immediately and put it away, we will give you another chance." Lincoln looked somewhat surprised and relieved, since he had been unaware of his own offense. Jennifer, then remembering and looking a little anxious, awaited her own instruction. Placing one arm around her little girl, her mother said, "Jennifer, my dear, we will need to ground you for a week, according to the family decision." To this seemingly unfair treatment Jennifer immediately resisted. And then from the scriptures lying open on the kitchen table, frayed and worn, their mother read to them from Matthew 7:2: "For with what judgment ye judge, ye shall be judged: and with what measure ye mete, it shall be measured to you again." Time was allowed for questions and for answers to whys, until even Jenny felt secure about the great confidence her mother expressed in her as she spoke of her unusual gifts and talents and her radiant personality that needed a little tempering.

And so by the end of the day this young mother was, as usual, probably behind in many things, but way ahead in others.

Preparing a Heart for the Spirit's Touch

JAMES M. HARPER

Eighteen-year-old Latter-day Saint young men struggle to decide about missions, some more than others. My son was no exception. We watched him go through this struggle, but when he turned nineteen, he filled out his papers, had his physical and dental exams, and made an appointment with our new bishop to turn in his mission papers. This was the bishop's first interview with a prospective missionary. My son returned from the interview with all his papers still in hand and announced: "I just told the bishop I am not going on a mission." I said nothing, at least knowing better than to be critical. I had learned that maybe I needed to look inside myself to find why this was so scary for me. His mother said something very interesting. "Son, we'll support whatever you choose to do," she said, "but far more important than how we feel about this as your parents is that you work out your relationship with Heavenly Father, with Christ as your mediator. So I ask only one thing of you. Make sure that you pray about this." I suppose my wife could have tried to convince our son that a mission was the best thing to do, reminding him of all the teachings in our family. Instead she chose to facilitate his own discovery and try to prepare his heart for the Spirit's touch in that prayer. A week later he went back to the bishop to turn in his papers.

This must have been quite a trial for our new bishop. He later shared with us what our son had told him: "You know, when I came in last week, I thought that the only reason I wanted to serve a mission was because my parents expected me to, but I've learned this week that my parents will support me no matter what I choose. Far more important, I've learned this week that the Lord expects me to serve a mission, and I need to do it to be of service to him."

He served his mission and has been home for several years. It changed his life in all the ways that missions do.

What Else Would He Forget?

ANITA R. CANFIELD

My ten-year-old son kept forgetting his lunch. Day after day, despite many reminders, I would find myself running up to the school at the lunch hour with the little brown bag. I even tried leaving it at the front door. The problem persisted, and I got cross with him; I pleaded with him, left notes. Nothing was working.

He began forgetting homework assignments and other small responsibilities. He was an energetic, normal ten-year-old, preoccupied with many other adventures like fort building, bicycling, and sports.

One morning I opened the refrigerator and saw the brown bag. As I looked it seemed to take other shapes: a future college term paper, a family in his mission, a career, his own wife and children, Church callings. Would these dependencies on someone else always rescuing him create larger problems in the future? Would his self-reliance be handicapped?

Slowly I closed the refrigerator door, lunch still inside.

I didn't eat lunch that day either. I thought of my little boy who loved his food. He never was hungry, he was always starving! I am sure the pain I felt was worse than the pain of his hunger. When he came in he stormed in, like a miniature tornado, wondering why I hadn't brought his lunch to him, he was starving! He opened the door and devoured it.

We spent the next few minutes talking about his responsibility to take care of his assignments in life. At ten years old he wasn't responsible for providing food for himself; his parents were. But at ten years old he was responsible to take his lunch to school. If he could learn to do this, he could be given greater, then greater responsibilities. But it was all his choice. I also assured him I wouldn't be bringing his lunch to school anymore.

He never forgot it again.

An Easy Unconditionality

VIRGINIA H. PEARCE

Editor's Note: The following selection comes from a book about Marjorie Pay Hinckley, wife of Church President Gordon B. Hinckley. Virginia H. Pearce is the third of President and Sister Hinckley's five children.

In all of Mother's relationships, there is an easy unconditionality. If you wipe the drainboards off in a different direction than she does, do your laundry differently, or approach a Relief Society lesson your own way, she expresses wonder and delight rather than making it a point to "help you do it right" the next time. Always words of admiration and validation. Never critical judgments. The net result: No one has to "perform." People can use all of their energy to get on with the business of living. Maybe this is what they call "unconditional love."

After I became an adult, I don't remember her ever telling me how I should or should not do things, being critical, or even giving advice. But I do remember one time when she offered a suggestion.

Unlike women of character, I have always been able to sleep quite comfortably at night with dirty dinner dishes all over the kitchen. After I've fixed and served dinner, I have just enough energy rationed out to do the "getting-the-kids-to-bed" routine. Barely. However, I have boundless morning energy, and I quite like whipping the kitchen into shape first thing.

Mother came to help me when my twins were born. After observing my habit of leaving the kitchen cluttered at night, as well as my inability to get a handle on the other housework, laundry, child care, and so on, she said: "Ginny, you might be better off if you just did the dishes at night. Then you could start every day with at least a clean kitchen." So unlike her was the comment that I remember exactly where both of us were standing when she made it. But, as unusual as it was, her voice still said that it was entirely my option. I didn't take the advice, and I don't believe she ever mentioned it again. It really shows your mettle as a teacher when you can offer an idea and then let go. And I don't think she was even biting her tongue.

"*I* Don't Know If I Have a Testimony"

MICHAELENE P. GRASSLI

One day Stephanie was riding in the car with her parents. She began to express some confusion over testimony. "I don't know if I have a testimony," she said. "I really don't know if the Church is true or not."

Her mother wisely replied: "A testimony is a good thing to wonder about, because it is a personal thing—only you can know what you believe. But let me help you remember some things that I think you might not know are part of your testimony. Do you remember when you and Eliza were talking about a lesson you had in Primary and you said it made both of you feel happy inside to talk about things you learned at Church?

"Another time we were in sacrament meeting and the speaker was telling us about prayer. He said that Heavenly Father hears our prayers and answers them. You turned to me and said, 'I know that too.'

"And then, one morning after we finished reading scriptures and had family prayer, you kept your scriptures open and reread the passages we had studied. I asked you what you were reading and you said, 'I feel warm inside when I read the scriptures.'

"Stephanie, each one of those experiences was the Spirit telling or confirming to you that the gospel of Jesus Christ is true."

Stephanie responded, "I guess I do have a testimony!" Then with excitement she related other experiences where she had received a confirmation of the Spirit.

"Now I Can Shake Hands with the Priesthood of God"

MATTHEW COWLEY

I had a little mother . . . down in New Zealand. I knew her on my first mission when I was just a young boy. In those days she called me her son. When I went back to preside, she called me her father. I am fearfully and wonderfully made.

Now, on one occasion I called in, as I always did when I visited that vicinity, to see this grand little woman, then in her eighties, and blind. She did not live in an organized branch, had no contact with the priesthood except as the missionaries visited there. We had no missionaries in those days. They were away at war.

I went in and greeted her in the Maori fashion. She was out in her back yard by her little fire. I reached forth my hand to shake hands with her, and I was going to rub noses with her, and she said: "Do not shake hands with me, Father."

I said: "Oh, that is clean dirt on your hands. I am willing to shake hands with you. I am glad to. I want to."

She said: "Not yet." Then she got on her hands and knees and crawled over to her little house. At the corner of the house there was a spade. She lifted up that spade and crawled off in another direction, measuring the distance she went. She finally arrived at a spot and started digging down into the soil with that spade. It finally struck something hard. She took out the soil with her hands and lifted out a fruit jar. She opened that fruit jar and reached down in it, took something out and handed it to me, and it turned out to be New Zealand money. In American money it would have been equivalent to one hundred dollars.

She said: "There is my tithing. Now I can shake hands with the priesthood of God."

I said: "You do not owe that much tithing."

She said: "I know it. I do not owe it now, but I am paying some in advance, for I do not know when the priesthood of God will get around this way again."

And then I leaned over and pressed my nose and forehead against hers, and the tears from my eyes ran down her cheeks, and as I left her, I asked God in my heart to bring down upon me a curse if from that day henceforth and forever I did not return to God . . . one-tenth of all that should ever come into my hands.

Five Lessons of Love

ELAINE CANNON

I once had to shut myself and our four little ones under six into the nursery. I had a fever of 104 degrees, and I was pregnant again. Staying upright was no longer a viable option. In my misery I curled up on a youth bed to keep a watchful eye on our precious destroying angels. Balls and baby bottles sailed over my head while dark thoughts stirred my mind. My young husband was a conscientious new bishop who was always visiting the sick, and I wondered how sick one had to be to get the bishop to come and call in our home!

I didn't feel like much of a mother—more like a big baby, such was my self-pity.

Then the doorbell rang, and I dragged from the bed to peer through the window to the front porch. There stood the Relief Society president, an older woman who worked closely with my young husband in the welfare needs of our ward. She was old enough to be my mother, and I was appalled that she should catch me in my failure, in this house of chaos where no mother's hand had been raised recently to do more than keep the little ones from hurting each other.

The stampede to answer the doorbell came from children aching for release from the confinement of the nursery. While I called through the window that I was ill and would see her another time, the children were already opening the door for her.

Then the most marvelous bit of "other mothering" occurred. This time I was the child being taught lifesaving lessons. This fine friend explained that she had been driving by our house and had felt prompted by the Spirit that help was needed therein.

Lesson one: Be in tune and respond to the promptings of the Spirit.

She had hurried home to get her ever-ready Friendship Bag, full of supplies and surprises for the sick and afflicted.

Lesson two: Be prepared and equipped to meet the need.

Returning to our home, she rang the doorbell until there was a response.

Lesson three: Don't give up too soon in doing your good deeds!

She told me to lie down on the living room couch while she lured the children to the kitchen table with cookies and new coloring books. She would help me in a moment. In relief, I obeyed.

Lesson four: Even a mother needs a mother on occasion.

Sister Jensen took my foot in her hands, ignoring my protests of embarrassment that she would be doing that to *me!* She talked quietly and comfortingly, all the while massaging each foot while she healed my soul. There was quiet for a moment, and then I got lesson five: "Love your partner, Elaine. Love him enough so that he has plenty to give his ward members. Let your bishop-husband be a good shepherd."

"That's All Right"

BROOKIE PETERSON

Millie came from a large family. Her mother's life was one of hard work, and included the mammoth chore of cooking for many people.

One day when Millie was a girl of about twelve the family was going to eat outside in the yard. The mother had had a busy day but had prepared a tasty meal, the main dish being a large kettle of stew. Most of the family was gathered outside when the mother asked Millie to bring out the kettle of savory meat and vegetables. As Millie walked out with it she stumbled and spilled the food on the ground. All the children looked at their mother. After a brief moment, during which she took a deep breath, Millie's mother spoke as she might have spoken to a treasured friend. "That's all right, Millie. Those things happen sometimes."

She made a lifetime memory in the mind of every child present.

Christmas Story

KATHLEEN "CASEY" NULL

I wanted the shopping trip to be perfect. That's why I planned it two weeks in advance. No more last-minute, slip-shod gift giving by any of my kids . . . no way.

I sat them down and had them make lists. Oh, sure, they groaned about it. But if they didn't make lists, it would be just like all the other Christmases.

One would go off to a shopping center with six dollars and spend a dollar twenty-five on gifts for two parents, three siblings, four grandparents, and one dog, and spend the remaining four seventy-five on gum and darts for himself.

The other would be conned out of most of his allowance by his brother. And another would lose his money down the heater vents.

I took their allowance—carefully sorted into labeled envelopes—their lists, and them to the mall.

"Maul" would be a better name for it.

Christmas is for families but Christmas shopping is better accomplished by individuals—unless you're willing to invest in some mountain-climbing equipment and leash the family all together. Even my daughter in a large stroller got separated from me when I removed my hand to look at the list.

My four-year-old got stuck at the top of an escalator after a sudden attack of escalator-phobia. My one-year-old nearly got us arrested when she "shoplifted" a bottle of nail polish—it was an awful shade too. My eight-year-old kept twenty people waiting while the clerk counted out his seven dollars and twenty-nine cents in change, mostly pennies.

Shopping en masse was not working. Instead, I'd wait outside each store with my sticky-fingered daughter while two boys at a time would enter to shop. They'd come out and I'd inspect.

"What's this comic book for?"

"That's for Daddy."

"I thought you were getting him that pen that writes in three colors."

"I couldn't find one."

"What are these baby booties for? They're too small for Kiera."

"Christopher bought those."

"Michael! You shouldn't've let him."

"Mom! He started to cry in the middle of the store. He says they're for the baby Jesus."

"Okay," I sighed.

No, I decide. It's better than okay. Christopher's got a lesson to teach us. As I wait for Jason to come out I begin to imagine the possibilities of Christopher's lesson. We'll keep the booties for every Christmas; we'll put them under the tree or maybe by the Nativity scene. It will be an important family tradition. What a great idea!

Feeling full of fresh Christmas cheer, I let the kids take a cheese and cracker break. As we munched, a very-large-with-child young woman sank wearily onto a nearby bench.

Michael whispered loudly. "Mom? Is that lady going to have a baby?"

She heard. "Yes . . . pretty soon."

"A Christmas baby? Like baby Jesus?" Christopher asked. The woman smiled.

Christopher studied her for a long time.

Finally she got up to finish her shopping and Christopher ran after her with his baby booties.

"Here," he panted, "for the baby."

I wanted the shopping trip to be perfect. But I really didn't know what a perfect shopping trip it would be . . . until that moment.

The Daffodil Principle

JAROLDEEN ASPLUND EDWARDS

Several times my daughter had telephoned to say, "Mother, you must come see the daffodils before they are over." I wanted to go, but it was a two-hour drive from Laguna to Lake Arrowhead. Going and coming took most of a day—and I honestly did not have a free day until the following week.

"I will come next Tuesday," I promised, a little reluctantly, on her third call.

Next Tuesday dawned cold and rainy. Still, I had promised, and so I drove the length of Route 91, continued on I-215, and finally turned onto Route 18 and began to drive up the mountain highway.

The tops of the mountains were sheathed in clouds, and I had gone only a few miles when the road was completely covered with a wet, gray blanket of fog. I slowed to a crawl, my heart pounding.

The road becomes narrow and winding toward the top of the mountain. As I executed the hazardous turns at a snail's pace, I was praying to reach the turnoff at Blue Jay that would signify I had arrived.

When I finally walked into Carolyn's house and hugged and greeted my grandchildren, I said, "Forget the daffodils, Carolyn! The road is invisible in the clouds and fog, and there is nothing in the world except you and these darling children that I want to see bad enough to drive another inch!"

My daughter smiled calmly. "We drive in this all the time, Mother."

"Well, you won't get *me* back on the road until it clears—and then I'm heading for home!" I assured her.

"I was hoping you'd take me over to the garage to pick up my car. The mechanic just called, and they've finished repairing the engine," she answered.

"How far will we have to drive?" I asked cautiously.

"Just a few blocks," Carolyn said cheerfully. So we bundled up the children and went out to my car. "I'll drive," Carolyn offered. "I'm used to this."

We got into the car, and she began driving. In a few minutes I was aware that we were back on the Rim-of-the-World road heading over the top of the mountain.

"Where are we going?" I exclaimed, distressed to be back on the mountain road in the fog. "This isn't the way to the garage!"

"We're going to my garage the long way," Carolyn smiled, "by way of the daffodils."

"Carolyn," I said sternly, trying to sound as if I were still the mother and in charge of the situation, "please turn around. There is nothing in the world that I want to see enough to drive on this road in this weather."

"It's all right, Mother," she replied with a knowing grin. "I know what I'm doing. I promise, you will never forgive yourself if you miss this experience."

And so my sweet, darling daughter who had never given me a minute of difficulty in her whole life was suddenly in charge—and she was kidnapping me! I couldn't believe it. Like it or not, I was on the way to see some ridiculous daffodils—driving through the thick, gray silence of the mist-wrapped mountaintop at what I thought was risk to life and limb. I muttered all the way.

After about twenty minutes we turned onto a small gravel road that branched down into an oak-filled hollow on the side of the mountain. The fog had lifted a little, but the sky was lowering, gray and heavy with clouds. We parked in a small parking lot adjoining a little stone church. From our vantage point at the top of the mountain we could see beyond us, in the mist, the crests of the San Bernardino range like the dark, humped backs of a herd of elephants. Far below us the fog-shrouded valleys, hills, and flatlands stretched away to the desert.

On the far side of the church I saw a pine-needle-covered path, with towering evergreens and manzanita bushes and an inconspicuous, hand-lettered sign, "Daffodil Garden."

We each took a child's hand, and I followed Carolyn down the path as it wound through the trees. The mountain sloped away from the side of the path in irregular dips, folds, and valleys, like a deeply creased skirt. Live oaks, mountain laurel, shrubs, and bushes clustered in the folds, and in the gray, drizzling air, the green foliage looked dark and monochromatic. I shivered. Then we turned a corner of the path, and I looked up and gasped.

Before me lay the most glorious sight, unexpectedly and completely splendid. It looked as though someone had taken a great vat of gold and poured it down over the mountain peak and slopes, where it had run into every crevice and over every rise. Even in the mist-filled air, the mountainside was radiant, clothed in massive drifts and waterfalls of daffodils. The flowers were planted in majestic, swirling patterns, great ribbons and swaths of deep orange, white, lemon yellow, salmon pink, saffron, and butter yellow. Each different-colored variety (I learned later that there were more than thirty-five varieties of daffodils in the vast display) was planted as a group so that it swirled and flowed like its own river with its own unique hue.

In the center of this incredible and dazzling display of gold, a great cascade of purple grape hyacinth flowed down like a waterfall of blossoms framed in its own rock-lined basin, weaving through the brilliant daffodils. A charming path wound throughout the garden. There were several resting stations, paved with stone and furnished with Victorian wooden benches and great tubs of coral and carmine tulips.

As though this were not magnificence enough, Mother Nature had to add her own grace note—above the daffodils, a bevy of western bluebirds flitted and darted, flashing their brilliance. These charming little birds are the color of sapphires with breasts of magenta red. As they dance in the air, their colors are truly like jewels. Above the blowing, glowing daffodils, the effect was spectacular.

It did not matter that the sun was not shining. The brilliance of the daffodils was like the glow of the brightest sunlit day. Words, wonderful as they are, simply cannot describe the incredible beauty of that flower-bedecked mountaintop.

Five acres of flowers! (This too I discovered later when some of my questions were answered.) "But who has done this?" I asked Carolyn. I was overflowing with gratitude that she had brought me—even against my will. This was a once-in-a-lifetime experience. "Who?" I asked again, almost speechless with wonder, "and how, and why, and when?"

"It's just one woman," Carolyn answered. "She lives on the property. That's her home." Carolyn pointed to a well-kept A-frame house that looked small and modest in the midst of all that glory.

We walked up to the house, my mind buzzing with questions. On the patio we saw a poster. "Answers to the Questions I Know You Are Asking" was the headline. The first answer was a simple one. "50,000 bulbs," it read. The second answer was, "One at a time, by one woman. Two hands, two feet, and very little brain." The third answer was, "Began in 1958."

There it was. The Daffodil Principle. For me that moment was a life-changing experience. I thought of this woman whom I had never met, who, more than thirty-five years before, had begun—one bulb at a time—to bring her vision of beauty and joy to an obscure mountaintop.

One bulb at a time. There was no other way to do it. One bulb at a time. No shortcuts—simply loving the slow process of planting. Loving the work as it unfolded. Loving an achievement that grew so slowly and that bloomed for only three weeks of each year.

Still, just planting one bulb at a time, year after year, had changed the world. This unknown woman had forever changed the world in which she lived. She had created something of ineffable magnificence, beauty, and inspiration.

The principle her daffodil garden taught me is one of the greatest principles of celebration: learning to move toward our goals and desires one step at a time—often just one baby-step at a time—learning to love the doing, learning to use the accumulation of time. When we multiply tiny pieces of time with small increments of daily effort, we too will find we can accomplish magnificent things. We can change the world.

"Carolyn," I said that morning on the top of the mountain as we left the haven of daffodils, our minds and hearts still bathed and bemused by the splendors we had seen, "it's as though that remarkable woman has needle-pointed the earth! Decorated it. Just think of it, she planted every single bulb. For more than thirty years. One bulb at a time! And that's the only way this garden could be created. Every individual bulb had to be planted. There was no way of short-circuiting that process. Five acres of blooms. That magnificent cascade of hyacinth! All, all, just one bulb at a time." The thought of it filled my mind. I was suddenly overwhelmed with the implications of what I had seen.

"It makes me sad in a way," I admitted to Carolyn. "What might I have accomplished if I had thought of a wonderful goal thirty-five years ago and had worked away at it 'one bulb at a time' through all those years. Just think what I might have been able to achieve!"

My wise daughter put the car into gear and summed up the message of the day in her direct way. "Start tomorrow," she said with the same knowing smile she had worn for most of the morning. Oh, profound wisdom! It is pointless to think of the lost hours of yesterdays. The way to make learning a lesson a celebration instead of a cause for regret is to only ask, "How can I put this to use tomorrow?"

I also learned on that gray and golden morning what a blessing it is to have a child who is not a child anymore but a woman—perceptive and loving beyond her years—and to be humble in that awareness.

Thank you, Carolyn. Thank you for the lessons of that unforgettable morning. Thank you for the gift of the daffodils.

 Children

He Still Had His Old Ones

MICHAELENE P. GRASSLI

It was a bitter cold winter in southeast Idaho and eleven-year-old Kelly had barely had time to arrive at school when he telephoned his mother.

"Mom, could you bring my old coat to school, please?" he asked.

"Why, Kelly?"

"Because I gave my new one away."

His mother tried to remain calm. "You *what?*"

"Mom, one of the Indian boys from the reservation came this morning with no coat on, and Mom, his ears were frostbitten, and he was crying." The temperatures had been below zero. "Mom, he stood and waited for the bus for half an hour. I gave him my hat and my gloves too. I hope you don't mind. I knew I still had my old ones."

"𝓘 Always Do That"

SHERRIE JOHNSON

We should teach our children to listen for a few moments after their prayers are said. Listening is the most important part of prayer. It doesn't make any sense to ask for answers and then close our prayer and jump into bed. To get an answer to prayer we must listen to the promptings and feelings within us. The quiet moments of listening allow the Spirit to speak to us.

One night while kissing five-year-old Anissa good night, I started to review the process of how to pray and then listen, only to have her raise her little hand and interrupt. "I know, I know, I always do that," she said, waving her hand to stop me from saying more, "because once when I listened Heavenly Father said, 'I love you'!"

ʃtature

VESTA NICKERSON FAIRBAIRN

A minor scratch, a hurt, and the small disgrace
Of sudden tears is quickly gone
If a five-year-old is bandage glorified
When he emerges later on.

"Is the Book of Mormon True?"

MICHAELENE P. GRASSLI

Seven-year-old Eric and his family were being taught by the missionaries. After hearing about the Book of Mormon, Eric asked, "How can we know if it's true?" The missionaries asked him what he thought he could do to find out. "I guess I could ask God, and he'd tell me," came the response. At that point, the missionaries committed each member of the family to pray and ask God if the book was true.

As they finished the discussion, the missionaries asked if they could say a closing prayer. Little Eric said, "Why don't we pray right now to find out if the Book of Mormon is true?" And then he offered a simple prayer: "God, I want to thank you for the things we talked about. I'm excited about it, and I just want to know, is the Book of Mormon true?" Here there was a pause and the Spirit flooded in upon the little family. Then Eric continued, "I sure hope so because I feel really good inside." He had a desire to know. He had a desire to believe.

After the prayer, the missionaries invited all the family members to explain how they had felt during the prayer. They helped the family recognize that the Holy Ghost had witnessed to them that the answer Eric had prayed for had indeed been given to them.

"*I* Love You to Infinity"

GEORGE D. DURRANT

One little boy who wasn't yet in school had been listening to his older brothers and sisters discuss their mathematics. That night as his mother tucked him into bed he looked at her, kissed her good night, and said, "Mom, I love you to infinity."

"That's a pretty big word for such a little boy," his mother said. "Do you know what it means?"

"Sure I do, Mom," he replied. "It means I love you on and on forever."

$\mathcal{D}$ear Primary Teacher

KATHLEEN "CASEY" NULL

Dear Primary Teacher,

My very young son is in your class. Let me tell you about him.

He likes to say his prayers, but if he is asked to pray in front of others he will efficiently bless the food. So if you call on him to pray in class and hear him express gratitude for the food, thank him anyway. One day someone besides me will hear one of his eloquent and charming prayers; hopefully it will be you.

He is also very affectionate. Although he is a bit young to have such a preference for girls, and not old enough to have an aversion to them, I'd suggest that you seat him by other boys. He likes to kiss girls and wrestle with boys. I think you might be better prepared for wrestling boys than a lot of kissing.

Please keep in mind that three-year-olds have incredible imaginations. Don't believe a word he says about our personal family life.

Although we will frisk him before he enters your classroom, the inevitable Lego or ball bearing will get through anyway. Simply reassure him that his treasures will be returned to him soon as you slip them into your pocket.

You may need to remind him that he is to remain fully clothed until he gets home.

He will raise his hand and volunteer for anything. Please help him see that anyone can raise their hand, the important part is carrying it out.

Sometimes he will miss class because he is hovering between

babyhood and childhood. Please don't be offended. It takes time to let go of Mom and take the hand of a teacher.

He will cry in class from time to time. Don't be alarmed. He needs to find out if you can comfort him.

Although at home he has moments when he is careful and contemplative, in your classroom he is likely to be silly and scribble all over your handouts. Even three-year-olds are self-conscious and hide their true selves in a group situation.

A gentle touch from you and an encouraging word will assure him that he belongs. You will be rewarded by his devotion.

You may think he isn't learning a thing in your class with all the wrestling, kissing, scribbling, silliness, and undressing. But he is, I assure you. He remembers every word you say, every facial expression you make, every attitude you imply.

He is so young. He doesn't yet know what classrooms are all about. He is a tender stranger to adults who are not family members. Please keep in mind when he tips his chair over or has a tantrum because another boy got the brown crayon first, that he has only been on earth for three years. And he has so much to learn. And that parents who love him beyond his comprehension have entrusted him to your influence.

Music to the Ears

FRANCINE R. BENNION

Once, learning to play a Bach fugue, I sat at the piano managing for the first time to make all things work together towards a magnificent climax when my young son reached up to the keyboard to try to stop my fingers from moving.

"Mommy?"

"Just a minute, Brett. I'm just about finished."

"Mommy?"

"Wait a minute, please."

"Mommy?"

The climax ruined, I took my hands off the keyboard, expecting some trivial little question, and said impatiently, "What is it?"

"Mommy? Mommy, I love you."

"Listen to Me"

MARILYN JEPPSON CHOULES

As a young mother with five small children, I was busy at the kitchen counter fixing dinner. My young son Jimmy came running in and said, "Mom, Mom."

"Yes," I responded, as I continued working at the counter.

"Mom," he implored, "listen to me."

"I'm listening," I replied as I continued working.

"No," Jimmy said, "listen with your face!"

"Of Course We've Seen Him!"

MICHAELENE P. GRASSLI

My friend Jan, substituting in her son's Primary class, was teaching a lesson about faith. As Jan explained that we haven't seen Heavenly Father, but we believe in him and have faith in his existence, she noticed quizzical looks on the faces of the children in the class.

Finally Kara raised her hand and said, "But Sister Blackburn, we *have* seen Heavenly Father." Jan was taken aback momentarily. Kara added, "We lived with him once. Of course we've seen him!" There was no question in Kara's pure child heart and mind. She believed. And she was right, of course.

Confection Perfectionist

KATHLEEN "CASEY" NULL

I must have been daydreaming. I saw myself in a gingham apron surrounded by worshipful, apple-cheeked children and the aroma of bread and cinnamon.

It's those women's magazines. The Christmas issues get to me every time! All those lavish gingerbread houses, and the Christmas decorations painstakingly fashioned from discarded milk jugs and juice cans that had been saved, supposedly, all year long just for Christmas.

I succumb to their lure only once a year when Christmas baking, decorations, parties, and even clever gift wrapping become equated with love (in my mind or the magazine's, I'm not sure which, but I have my suspicions).

So I pore over those Christmas issues like a college freshman opening brand-new geology and sociology text books, with a mixture of dread and excitement.

Oh, no. They won't get me to stay up till midnight finishing a Victorian gingerbread house just because I love my kids. One of them would probably sit on it anyway.

And I am certainly not interested in putting together that wreath with 28,300 gum wrappers folded into intricate patterns and spray-painted gold, even though I could surely come up with the correct amount of gum wrappers by cleaning the boys' room. That's not love, that's obsession.

But the daydream persists. It is, after all, Christmas; and these are, after all, little children. I am responsible for their memories! Do I want them to tell my grandchildren about how I stopped off at the bakery on Christmas Eve? Are you kidding? I want them to wax poetic as they reminisce about the smells of evergreen and cloves and the taste of homemade goodies. These are warm manifestations of their mother's love, right?

The daydream returns. I see a patient, sweet mother in the kitchen with her children. They are making Christmas cookies together. One apple-cheeked boy has a smudge of flour on his button nose. Dad comes home and the scene before him fills his heart with joy. Now isn't that what Christmas is all about?

In an attempt to play the daydream out in real life I announce, "We're going to make Christmas cookies!"

My number one son says, "Aw, Mom, I want to go to Roger's; he's got video games."

The rest of the children shout "Goodie!" with so much glee that I wonder if they shouldn't be locked out of the kitchen.

I get out the flour. I get Christopher out of the flour. I get the flour out of Christopher's hands. I ask Michael to get the flour off the floor.

I get out the cookie cutters. I wash the play dough off the cookie cutters. Jason gets the rolling pin from the sandbox.

Finally we have the dough mixed. Half of it, however, has "mysteriously" disappeared.

Christopher holds up a gob of dough. "Can I eat this?"

I sigh, "You may as well."

He says, "Why?"

Jason rolls the dough. I answer the phone.

Christopher asks, "Why do I have to eat this?"

Michael says, "Mom, he's not letting me have a turn!"

The baby cries. I go to change her.

In the kitchen I hear the kind of commotion that makes mothers want to slip out of the back door.

I take a deep breath and go back.

I see raw cookies everywhere. Some are even on the cookie sheet, a few even cut with cookie cutters. Apparently that wasn't creative enough—the remainder have been formed by hand into oddly shaped monstrosities.

"This is a snake!"

"This is a monster!"

"This is Jabba the Hut!"

And I was going to wrap these gifts from our kitchen in gold foil and merrily deliver them to the neighbors.

I abandon all plans except for making it through the evening.

Frosting time has arrived and I'm gone again, putting the baby to bed. My three-year-old is following me around with that original piece of dough. "Is it good for me if I eat this?"

I decide that if I take out my contact lenses it will soften the shock of what I'll see when I return to the kitchen. I take another deep breath and plunge back in. When I left we had mixed several colors of frosting. Now all the cookies are being frosted with one color—a grayish green—which is, I am informed, "what you get when they're all mixed together."

I am weary of well doing. I rush the kids off to their beds and clean up.

Oh well, I can always stay up until midnight making banana bread for the neighbors.

Finally it's quiet. I look at those magazines again. Obviously their test kitchens don't include children. That would be a *real* test kitchen.

Three-year-old Christopher calls from the darkness. He wants a drink. I bring him into the kitchen. He puts his arms around my neck and asks, "Did you see my cookies?"

I tiredly nod. "Yes."

He says, "My Mary?"

"Your what?"

I look at the grayish blobs where he points.

"I made Mary and Joseph and the baby Jesus."

I look again and begin to see the forms shaped by his pudgy hands.

"Yes, I see, Christopher . . . they're wonderful."

We give each other a good-night hug.

I put him to bed and come back out and throw out those magazines.

Husbands and Fathers

What Love Is

JANENE WOLSEY BAADSGAARD

Love isn't always hearts and flowers and lace. For as far back as I can remember, I loved to curl up with an afghan and a good romance novel. The Brontë sisters' mist-covered English moors were my second home. I brought many of those romantic ideals to my marriage. As the years went by, my husband didn't seem to measure up to those ideals, and I sometimes felt I was missing something.

Our neighbors, a young couple married about the same time we were, only reinforced my dilemma. I found myself wanting the same honeymoon-like relationship I thought they had.

One Valentine's Day, I decided to throw enough hints at my husband to instantly change him into the romantic hero I envisioned. Things didn't work out the way I planned.

"What are you doing?" he asked as he sat down at the breakfast table.

"Making valentine cookies."

"Why are you doing that?" He handed the baby his bottle and poured some cereal for our impatient two-year-old.

"It's Valentine's Day," I announced. "Happy Valentine's Day, sweetheart." I leaned over and kissed his cheek.

"Oh. Happy Valentine's Day. Where's the sugar?"

"Right here," I said, a little disheartened but not defeated. "I saw a florist's truck stop in front of the Andersons' house this morning."

My husband wasn't paying much attention.

"Seems as though Mr. Anderson is always giving flowers to his wife. Those Andersons are really romantic, aren't they?"

"What did you say, dear?" he asked, wiping up the milk our three-year-old had just spilled.

"Oh, nothing," I replied, feeling a little discouraged.

My husband hurriedly put three more spoonfuls of cereal in his mouth, then stood up and announced, "Better get." He tucked in his shirt and wiped the spilled milk off his pants. "I put the diapers in the washing machine and fixed the kids' music box," he said as he took me in his arms and planted a kiss on my forehead. "Oh, and if Mr. Haring gets drunk and locks himself out of his apartment again before I get home, call the police. I had a spare key made for him and left it down at the station."

Later, as I was washing the breakfast dishes, I saw another florist's truck stop outside the Andersons' house. I watched wistfully as the deliveryman delivered a second red rose. Every hour thereafter a truck stopped in front of the Andersons' house and another red rose was delivered.

The children were helping me decorate valentine cookies with icing and candy when the doorbell rang. My heart started pounding when I opened the door and saw the deliveryman standing there smiling, holding a single red rose.

He didn't forget, I thought. "Thank you very much," I said as I reached out for the flower.

"Oh, I'm sorry," the deliveryman apologized. "This is for the lady across the street. Would you mind taking it over to her when she gets home?"

"Oh, of course not," I said.

I put the rose on the kitchen table, where we were working on the cookies, and stared at it. The baby cried. Then I cried.

When I heard a car door slam across the street, I herded all my preschoolers together, and we marched over with the rose.

"Mrs. Anderson," I said as she opened the door, "the florist brought this by earlier and asked me to run it over to you."

She took the rose and, without even looking at it, put it on the floor of her entry along with the others that had been delivered earlier. She looked like a model who had just stepped out of a fashion magazine.

"May I hold the baby for a minute?" she asked.

I wiped his nose and let her take him.

"If you'll come in here," she said, pointing to the kitchen, "I have a surprise for you children."

They danced in front of her and nearly tripped her in their eagerness. She laughed as she regained her balance and opened the cookie jar. She pulled out several lollipops and handed them to my children. The baby greedily grabbed his candy, licked it, patted it, and put his sticky fingers in Mrs. Anderson's perfectly styled hair.

"Oh, dear," I said, embarrassed, "I'd better take him."

"I don't mind," she said, tickling the baby and smiling. "I don't get much chance to hold babies. My husband says children make him nervous," she added. "He says he wants it to stay just the way it is, just the two of us."

"Well, he sure is romantic," I said, pointing to the roses.

"I suppose he is," she replied as she reluctantly handed me the baby. "But I'm not the only woman he lavishes so much attention on. Sometimes I think all these flowers are just his way of making himself feel better about all the hours he spends away from me at the office or at the club."

That afternoon the baby grew fussy. He wouldn't nap, and he cried all afternoon. When I felt his forehead, he was burning up with fever.

"Where is your father?" I fumed as the afternoon grew into evening.

Finally my husband bounded through the front door, shaking snow off his shoes.

"Where have you been?" I said, staring at him.

"Sorry," he answered. "A man on the road had car trouble. I stopped and—" Then he looked at the baby. "What's the matter?"

"The baby's sick," I said, "really sick. I can't seem to settle him down."

"It's late," he said lovingly. "Let me take him. You go to bed."

Just before dawn I woke with a start. I couldn't remember hearing the baby cry all night. I ran out to the living room. My husband nodded in the rocking chair, the baby sleeping peacefully on his shoulder. The vaporizer, hissing from a corner of the room, filled the air with a moist fragrance.

As I stood there, with my worn, wrinkled flannel nightgown tumbling over my seven-months-pregnant stomach, I suddenly realized that love isn't the hearts and flowers and lace I had supposed it to be. At that moment, it was diaper pails being lifted into the washing machine, a stranded motorist who'd been befriended, a spare key at the police station, and a very red-eyed human being slouched in my squeaky rocking chair with a sick baby sleeping peacefully at his shoulder.

$\mathscr{A}$ Father's Support

ANITA R. CANFIELD

One evening in the Las Vegas Temple I witnessed a victory, a special victory that had to be born from courage that comes from keeping one's eye looking forward, focused on the Savior.

It was an unusual session in the fact that there were several individuals present with various disabilities. For example, one woman's feet were in special bandages, perhaps from some sort of surgery. There was also an elderly gentleman who was deaf. A television with closed caption had been brought in and placed in the front of the room for him. But the person who seemed the most handicapped was a very young man, about the age of a missionary, who was using a walker and was also being assisted by a man who appeared to be his father.

The young man, not much more than a boy really, seemed to struggle with each movement. He could not stand on his own and appeared to have tremendous difficulty in moving his limbs. I saw him a few days later at a wedding reception and learned who he was and what had happened to him.

He was a returned missionary. While snowboarding in Utah one Saturday, he had an accident that literally broke his neck. He was not supposed to live. In fact, there were some moments when his family thought he was indeed going to die. But he didn't. The prognosis was that he would never walk again. But he is walking. And I had the privilege of seeing where it was he wanted to walk to. He wanted to return to the temple.

That night in the temple, before I knew who he was, I watched his face. It seemed to me he was at such peace, a peace that surpassed his youth and his obviously painful ordeal. He looked so extremely happy to be there that night.

Near the end of the session, an invitation was extended to those who wanted to participate in a prayer circle. This young man was helped up on his walker by his father, and together they went up to the prayer circle. The television monitor had to be moved and a chair pushed aside to make room as he awkwardly made his way to the group. His father supported his arm and steadied the way.

Then I saw the special moment. Instead of joining the circle or returning to his seat, this loving father stepped behind his son. With both of his arms he reached out and wrapped them around his son's chest and under his arms. The boy let go of the walker so he could stand as he participated in the prayer. His father threw his entire strength into holding up his son so that he could be a part of this beautiful occasion.

It was one of the most touching scenes I have ever seen—a vivid portrayal of how great the Savior's and the Father's love is for us.

This young man had been through a grievous ordeal, a personal stormy sea. But he had not allowed himself to be distracted by the winds of adversity; rather, he had focused firmly on the Savior. He had wanted to return to the temple as part of his goals. He was walking on the turbulent waters to "go to Jesus." He was walking!

I saw the victory and much more. I saw a sweet metaphor of our Savior's love. If we will look to him, he will be there. He will support us; he will encircle us and sustain us, even if we can't see him. He will always remember us.

"Plant Onions"

MARION D. HANKS

Sitting across a table from me in a mission interview was a lovely girl to whom I had just said: "Sister, I wish I had an hour to talk with you, or half an hour, but I don't. I have about ten minutes, and then I must go to catch an airplane to keep faith with other people in other places. Knowing that you are finishing your mission, and having had a chance to just look in your eyes for a minute, I know there is something you could tell me that I ought to hear." She looked surprised, and she smiled to see if I was kidding. I wasn't. She thought for half a minute and then told me. In many ways it is the favorite thing I have heard in years and years. I give you only the headline:

Two brothers on missions, she a senior in college and earning her own way. A musician, a lovely person, she had decided she couldn't heed the promptings of the Spirit which were telling her that she was to go on a mission. She hadn't really ever contemplated it; her brothers were there. Her dad ran a little farm in Idaho which he had scratched over, sacrificed for, leased some of, and sold some of to keep her older brothers on missions. She just knew there wasn't anything left to sell or lease or anyplace else to get any money, and that her dad would insist on helping her if she went. So she just decided against it.

In her final year she went home for Christmas as usual, sat in the old front room in the old rocking chair looking at her father with that line across his forehead where his hat fit, noting the old suit and the gnarled hands, and her eyes welled with tears. She saw the threadbare carpet and thought of her mother in that old blue cloth coat, the one she'd had for years. And as they rocked they talked, until finally her father said, "Sweetheart, do you really want to go on a mission?"

"Daddy," she said, "we never talked about a mission."

"I know," he said. "Do you really want to go on a mission?"

"Daddy," she said, "I know that Bob and Bruce are on missions and that you don't have the money, and that you'd insist on helping me. And I know you can't sacrifice any more, and I don't intend to permit you to. I haven't any thought of going on a mission, Father."

After a pause he smiled and said, "Sweetheart, do you really want to go on a mission?"

She cried and said, "Yes, Daddy."

He said: "Then I'll tell you a story. When the Lord told me you wanted to go on a mission quite a while ago, I went out into the field, having fasted and prayed, and talked to Him. I said, 'Lord, my sweetheart wants to go on a mission and I have to have the privilege of helping her. How am I going to do it?' He said, 'Plant onions.' I said, 'How's that?' He said, 'Plant onions.' I said, 'I guess I'd better talk with you later, Lord.'"

He went home, worked the fields that day, fasted some more, and the next morning talked with the Lord again. " 'Lord, may I make myself perfectly clear. I've got to have a way to make some money to help my beautiful daughter. How am I going to do it?' And the Lord said, 'Plant onions.' I said, 'Yes, sir.' I went home, bought some seed [borrowed the money to do it], planted the seed, and began to pray and cultivate the crop. The Lord tempered the elements to the crop. It was a bountiful harvest. Others just don't grow onions around here. It's just too far north, too cold, usually. I sold the crop at a good price, paid my tithing, paid back what I'd borrowed, paid the taxes, and put the rest of it in the bank for you."

He went over to a drawer, got out a brand new bank book with one name on it—hers—and one entry for several thousand dollars, and said, "The Lord has provided for your mission."

She said, "Brother Hanks, I don't have any trouble believing

in a God who loves us and understands our needs and in His wisdom will provide for them, because I have that kind of a father."

Serving Mother

MARILYN JEPPSON CHOULES

Some years ago I learned that one of the sisters I visited as a visiting teacher needed to stay in bed for the remaining five months of her sixth pregnancy. My partner and I organized and made sure the family had meals brought in for several days.

Then I received a call from her husband. He said: "We appreciate the wonderful meals we have been enjoying. Our children have felt the love and kindness of the ward family. We are so grateful. However, I need to have you stop. My wife has sacrificed and served our family. This is a great opportunity for me to help our children learn to serve her. They will appreciate her much more as they learn to do for her many of the tasks she has done for them."

I have since moved from that ward, but later I saw that mother at a mall with her oldest daughter, who was pushing her own oldest child in a stroller. They were laughing and chatting together. What a picture of mutual love and kindness!

Little Wrangles

EDGAR A. GUEST

... We've had our little wrangles, an' we've had our little bouts;
There's many a time, I reckon, that we have been on the outs;
My tongue's a trifle hasty an' my temper's apt to fly,
An' Mother, let me tell you, has a sting in her reply,
But I couldn't live without her, an' it's plain as plain can be
That in fair or sunny weather Mother needs a man like me.

I've banged the door an' muttered angry words beneath my
breath,
For at times when she was scoldin' Mother's plagued me most to
death,
But we've always laughed it over, when we'd both cooled down
a bit,
An' we never had a difference but a smile would settle it.
An' if such a thing could happen, we could share life's joys an'
tears
An' live right on together for another thousand years.

Some men give up too easy in the game o' married life;
They haven't got the courage to be worthy of a wife;
An' I've seen a lot o' women that have made their lives a mess,
'Cause they couldn't bear the burdens that are mixed with
happiness.
So long as folks are human they'll have many faults that jar,
An' the way to live with people is to take them as they are.

We've been forty years together, good an' bad, an' rain an' shine;
I've forgotten Mother's faults now an' she never mentions mine.

In the days when sorrow struck us an' we shared a common woe
We just leaned upon each other, an' our weakness didn't show.
An' I learned how much I need her an' how tender she can be
An' through it, maybe, Mother saw the better side o' me.

Drastic Measures

JANENE WOLSEY BAADSGAARD

Couples with children in the home quickly find that they take a great deal of time and attention. But someday each child will leave the home to be married or to pursue his own life's work.

Our relationship with our children is important, but the relationship between husband and wife is the most sacred, the most intimate, and the most important human relationship in this life. Any effort we give that relationship will have eternal consequences.

Within a few years after our marriage, I recognized a craving to talk to someone over the age of four. My husband's response to my pleas for conversation was a brief glance above the newspaper or a polite nod during TV commercials. He simply couldn't see what was happening to our once adept ability to communicate and the spontaneous romantic experiences we had enjoyed early in our marriage. Drastic measures were called for.

When he walked in the door after work one night, I greeted him with "When will you ever learn to close the door behind you? Have you got mud on your shoes? Hang up your coat!"

When he sat down to supper, I interrupted him with "Go wash your hands!"

At the table, I poured him half a glass of milk and said, "Now, don't spill it. Where's your bib?"

I cut up his meat in tiny pieces and praised him when he managed to get a whole spoonful of food to his mouth without spilling. When he reached for his dessert, I caught his hand and said sternly, "No, no. You eat those yummy beets, or no dessert for you."

At bedtime, I tried to help him say his prayers. When we went to bed, as he put his arms around me, I turned to him and asked, "Did you go potty yet?"

"Janene," he said, "I've been thinking lately that maybe you and I could use a little more time to be alone together. How about a date Friday night?"

That was the beginning of our attempt to try to rekindle the old spark in our marriage. Every bit of effort we have put back into our relationship has really paid off.

Every couple owe each other continued courtship even after the babies start coming. A couple are first a husband and wife, then a father and mother. One of the nice things about putting each other first is that happy husbands and wives generally make better and happier fathers and mothers. That's a good recipe to remember: Happy Mom and Dad—Happy children.

"*I* Heard You"

ANITA R. CANFIELD

A father shared his testimony that the prayers of the Lord's people reach heaven. His five-year-old son was hospitalized, severely ill with encephalitis while the father was away from home for several weeks to manage five businesses. The father called several times a day. He visited with his wife and family, the bishop, and home teachers by phone. His grief overwhelmed him. He was desperate to be with his son and was frustrated because he could not.

He began to pray. He prayed unceasingly and without doubt. He petitioned the Lord to look after his family and if it was His will to restore his son to health. The more earnestly he prayed, the more he wanted to pray. He felt close to the Lord, to his child, to his family.

The son did recover and was released from the hospital about three weeks later. Shortly after that the father returned home. He spent time holding his son and expressing his love. Then he asked, "Stevie, what was it like being in the hospital so long? How did you feel?"

The little boy was thoughtful and then answered, "Daddy, I *heard* you."

"You heard me? What do you mean, Stevie, you *heard* me?"

"Daddy, I heard you. I heard you praying for me."

And then he repeated to this devoted father the very words he had prayed in behalf of his son. The little boy told him it helped him not to be afraid.

The Decision

MARION D. HANKS

Let me share with you the story of a beautiful soul in a troubled body. My wife and I met her as she received an award designated for one who had done the most to help the handicapped. From the moment of her birth, she had suffered a serious lack of normal physical blessings, but she had a great heart, a great spirit, and a great soul. In accepting the award, she recalled the day when she had run home from school crying because thoughtless, careless children had called her "hunchback" and other names. Her great father had held her in his arms and rocked her on his lap and wept with her as he impressed on her the importance of this day in her life.

"Elayne," he said to her, "today you decide. Your life can be all that God intends it to be. When they called you those names the boys and girls were in a sense telling the true facts. You do have a hump on your back and you have other problems that have made your life difficult physically. But, Elayne, as you were forming in your mother Heavenly Father knew that would be so. He sent a beautiful, special spirit, one that could handle the problems this little body would have. Now, Elayne, what they said about you is in a sense true, but it wasn't fair and it wasn't kind. If all your life you will be more fair and more kind to others than a few of them will sometimes be to you, then you will have a happy, warm, fruitful life, lack nothing, and be everything God intended."

And that beautiful little soul, who stood there with an oxygen tank behind her to help her breathe, who had to be helped to the platform, bore testimony of gratitude and love for God and her fellowman. She said, "The only real justification that I have for receiving this award is that I can say to you in honesty that all my life I have tried to be more fair and more kind to others than a few of them have sometimes been to me."

Ah, Alone!

KATHLEEN "CASEY" NULL

My husband and I went out on a date the other night. That's newsworthy.

We don't often have such an opportunity, what with six jobs, four Church callings, and four children between the two of us.

But we went. We actually walked out on all that and went to dinner and a movie.

It's not the same as it was when we were single. There was no time for the car-washing, hair-curling, and fancy-dressing rituals. There wasn't even time to change. We just slipped out of the door in jeans and running shoes, grateful for the chance.

Our baby-sitter, however, was nicely groomed.

I must admit that we did stop off at a shopping center to pick up some laundry detergent and baby cereal. You might think that's not a very romantic thing to do on a date, but hand holding in the condiments aisle can be wonderful . . . comparatively.

At the restaurant we felt funny. It was almost boring just sitting, talking, and eating. Boring but nice. We sat at the edge of our seats, ready for disaster, out of habit. If anyone had choked on food, we would've been the first to assist.

In the booth next to us there was a kid who reminded us of our three-year-old.

After dinner we browsed around some shops while waiting for our movie to begin. I kept looking behind me as I walked, and my husband looked at me strangely but didn't say anything.

Once I even blurted out, "Hurry up, there's a car coming!" Then he *really* looked at me strangely.

We looked in windows.

"Oh, wouldn't that be perfect for Kiera?"

"Yes, and wouldn't the boys love that?"

At one point I dropped my purse. It was so light without the usual diapers, bottles, burp rags, cars, and trucks that I forgot I had it.

"Oopsie!" I exclaimed, before I could stop myself.

"Oopsie"? I got the strangest look then.

One of the boys in the film reminded us of our eldest. The baby in the film was the same age as our baby.

After the film we tried not to talk about the kids, so we critiqued the film, the actors, and the plot. We discovered symbolism to discuss. We correlated the film's message with contemporary thought. As we approached our street we grew silent.

Inside, all were angelically sleeping except the baby. She leaped up at seeing us walk in the door.

Later we debated over the second best part of the evening.

We were unanimous about the best part—coming home.

Struggle and Sacrifice

$\mathcal{C}$hurch Time

JANENE WOLSEY BAADSGAARD

I know why the men in our church have so many meetings. It's so they won't have to go home and help get the kids ready for church.

Most Mormon moms have the glorious opportunity of orchestrating the frantic race to get to church on time. And most church schedules are arranged so that mothers of young children develop early ulcers.

If you're lucky enough to get the early schedule, you have to get up with the chickens and fly. You drag your sleepy-eyed children out of bed and try to get them to hurry. (By the way, children have no idea what *hurry* means.) You can always tell which children have the early schedule at church. Their hair looks like someone took an eggbeater to it, then sprayed it with Elmer's Glue.

If you get the middle schedule, you spend your time trying to decide if you should feed the kids lunch at 10:00 A.M. so you can make it to church at 11:00, or whether to wait until you get home at 2:00. Of course, the first alternative means the kids won't eat because they're not hungry, and the latter alternative means your young children will turn into raving monsters during sacrament meeting.

If you get the late schedule, forget about naps. You get to shake your child awake, then drag this delightful companion with you to church and spend three hours keeping him quiet. Of course, no self-respecting baby would be caught dead falling asleep at church. That would make it too easy for Mom.

Once you know when your meeting is supposed to start, your

next challenge is to get there. Why do mothers with young children look as if they've just been through a war when they walk through the doors of the chapel?

They have.

The other day, I hurriedly tried to get my three-year-old ready for church on time. I still had the other two children to get ready and only five minutes to do it in.

My three-year-old sat leisurely down by her shoe box, calmly measuring the pros and cons of two pairs of dressy shoes.

"What's the matter with you?" I said impatiently. "Hurry up!"

She didn't seem to listen to me as she slowly rubbed her small index finger over the toe of each shoe.

"These are too slickery," she said, "but these make my feet too squished." Then she noticed a toy truck next to her on the floor. She picked it up and made a vroom sound as she rolled the truck up and down the shoe box.

"Don't you know how to hurry?" I asked, my voice rising noticeably in volume.

My three-year-old looked at me, puzzled. She tried to stand up, but tripped over her shoes.

"We're going to be late! We're going to be late!" I chanted. "If you don't hurry up, we're going to be late!"

My three-year-old wrinkled her nose and peered at me, fascinated with my animated facial gestures and agitated tone of voice. Then she put her arms up in the air and stretched leisurely as she yawned.

I quickly walked over to her, picked her up off the floor, and sat her down briskly on the bed next to me. At that point, my four-year-old ran into the bedroom, her face covered with raspberry jam, and announced cheerfully, "I think the baby did something suspicious in his pants, Mom. He sure is stinky."

My three-year-old put her arm around me as I quickly finished buckling her shoes and said, "Mom, what's *hurry* mean?"

Getting to church is only part of the problem. Keeping the kids quiet once you get there is another part.

Every ward or branch has one Polly Perfection who sews the

family look-alike dresses and bow ties. They sit together on the front row, of all places, looking like an *Ensign* magazine cover. None of her children have coloring books, Cheerios, or quiet books. Her baby doesn't stomp Dinky Doughnut presweetened cereal into the carpet for the janitor to get mad about. Her baby sits up straight on her lap and listens to the speakers . . . even on High Council Sunday.

I am, of course, the mother standing up in the overflow section jiggling my baby up and down like a hot potato.

I guess I must have done something wrong in the pre-existence, the punishment for which was the curse of a buzzer bottom. As long as I stand up, my baby is fine. But just let me try to sit down and: "WAAAAAAA!" I think it works something like those dog whistles that have a high frequency sound that humans can't hear, but it sends dogs wild.

When my baby starts to fuss at the quietest moment of the service, I pick her up and try to soothe her. It doesn't work. I'm sitting on the buzzer, you see. So I get up and walk to the back of the church.

Soon, baby is sleeping soundly on my shoulder, even snoring. Slowly I edge myself back up to our bench and slowly, ever so slowly, I lower myself back into the seat. But as soon as I touch bottom . . . "WAAAAAAA!"

I wish someone would tell me how to unplug the thing.

Was It Worth It?
A Letter to My Wife, Marilyn

GEORGE D. DURRANT

We were married many years ago on an icy cold winter's day in mid-January. Recently, in speaking of that day, you jokingly said, "I'd never do that again."

"Sure you would," I replied.

"Don't be too sure," was your response.

"Look at where we are in life. We've had some real successes. And look at our children. Don't you think it has all been worth it?"

"Oh, sure, when you look at what we've done and our children. Then I know it's been a wonderful life. But we've sure had some hard times along the way. At least I have felt they were hard times."

I could tell that you were in a reflective mood, and as I thought back through the years, I sensed that at times life is indeed difficult, especially for a wife and mother. In an effort to show understanding I softly said, "You always amazed me at how you did what you did. I saw you get discouraged, I heard you cry, I saw you weakened by physical strain. I saw your worried concern but I never saw you give up. You never turned away. You always turned toward the center of things and walked directly into the action. You have been a tough woman, Marilyn."

I smiled as I added, "You told me once that if the man had to give birth to every other child, the largest number of children in any family would be three."

I remember a letter you wrote to me when our family was younger. In it you wrote: "George, you just don't realize how difficult things are for me. I know that you try, but there are so many things that you don't understand because you don't experience them. With Matt, Kathryn, Devin, Marinda, and Dwight still so young, and as I near the time of the birth of our new baby, I sometimes wonder if it is all worth it. Sometimes with all the demands on me and the physical and emotional strain involved, I wonder if I can make it.

"You are busy in your work and in your church assignments and you are so proud of our little family that you can't quite see that I need more of your help and love. Most of all, I need your understanding.

"I can tell that sometimes when you come home from work you are a little disgusted that the house is a little cluttered. I sense that you wonder what I've been doing all day.

"I snap at the children for some little thing they do wrong and you look at me like I am a tyrant. I feel like a tyrant. I don't want to be ornery with you and them. It's just that at times I feel like a failure as a wife and a mother and even as a human being."

You closed the letter by appealing to me that we sit down and talk about things. I remember that as we talked it seemed to help. I got the feeling that the best way I could help you during those difficult years was to be with you and talk to you. Yet so often I reacted in just the opposite way.

I remember the time in Brigham City when the children cried most of the night. Because I had a very important meeting early the next morning in Salt Lake City, I felt I'd better get a good night's rest. So when the children would wake up I'd remain in bed while you attended to their needs. After all, I reasoned, all you had to do the next day was stay home with the children.

When morning came I slipped quietly out of bed so as not to wake you or the children. I began to get dressed and discovered that I did not have a white shirt that was ironed. As I plugged in the iron to try to iron only those parts of the shirt that would show under my coat, I wondered, "What does Marilyn do all day?"

As I began to prepare my own breakfast I discovered there was no bread. I felt a slight twinge of disgust as I wondered, "How could she forget something as important as buying or baking a loaf of bread?" I hurriedly made hot cakes. I love hot cakes and I didn't have time to follow the recipe. "I know what goes in hot cakes," I said to myself as I cracked an egg into a cup of milk. Soon I was ready to eat. I took the first bite and was repulsed at the taste of what I had created.

By now my disgust was fully mature. I wanted you to know that I was completely displeased with your performance. Usually the best way I could do that was to be silent and not speak to you. On those occasions you'd sense I was upset and ask, "What is wrong?" I'd reply with an unpleasant, "Nothing is wrong," and again become silent. But, with you not there to observe my disgusted silence, all the negative emotion I was feeling was being wasted.

It was then that I decided that silence wouldn't work. I decided to bang around. The best time to bang around—move a chair, throw pans in a cupboard, and so on—is in the silence of early morning. I was sure that if I banged around, you would wake up and say to yourself, "George is banging around. I must have done something wrong."

Finally, when it was time to leave, I came back into the bedroom. I got my suit coat from the closet and put it on. Then I decided that if I really slid the sliding door hard, it would make the loudest bang of all. You'd really know then that I was upset.

I slid the door. Bang! Now you'd know. To cinch my message I'd leave the bedroom and the house without saying good-bye. Then you'd really know that I was upset and that you needed to do better as a wife and mother.

In that mental state I went to my office to get some papers for my meeting in Salt Lake. Because of the journey and the importance of the meeting I knelt to pray. As I did so, all I could think of was you. I said, "Heavenly Father, please bless Marilyn that she will have a happy day!" Then it seemed that I heard a voice say, "George, you go back home and bless her yourself—you are much closer than I am."

I ran back to my car and drove the few blocks back home. By now you were out of bed. Something had awakened you earlier. It took courage for me to do it, but I said, "Marilyn, I'm sorry."

Then I said something that was easier to say after what I'd just said. I added, "And I love you." I gave you a kiss and as I went out the door I shouted back, "I sure hope you have a happy day."

I relate that story to you now because it is symbolic of so much of our lives during the difficult years when our children were young. You had so much to do and needed my understanding, and yet at times I was caught up in my own needs and often failed to reach out and help you.

I remember that when we did sit down to talk you explained: "I feel bad that at times I get discouraged. It's just that on top of other things we have so many bills and that worries me. Our car is always breaking down and we can't afford any luxuries. I want to talk to you about these things more than we do, but I can tell that all that does is discourage you. I don't want to add any burdens to you because I know that you're doing your best. You need a cheerful, energetic wife. But at the same time, I need to be so many things that are difficult for me to be." You continued: "I see other women who apparently are far happier than me. Their homes seem neater, their clothes nicer, their interests more varied. At times I wonder if we are really going the right way, and if my sacrifices are worth it."

As I heard these remarks I must have looked quite sober, for you said: "But there are bright spots, and I really would not trade places with anyone in the world. I am always proud of you and I am grateful that you try so hard to be a good man and a good father. The children are cute because they look like my side of the family. They are good most of the time, and I am deeply grateful to be their mother. When we take them to church and other places, I'm proud to have them all there. Family home evenings are a joy to me because you do the teaching."

I smiled and felt better as you continued: "Family prayer helps. And dreaming about what the children can become brings sunshine into my heart. I feel that each of the children is special. It's hard for me not to brag. That's why I like to visit your mother. I can sit and brag to her about you, her son, and about our children, her grandchildren. She is probably the only one I can tell the truth to without worrying about people thinking I am boasting about my family."

Yes, those days that came and went so quickly were difficult but critical years for you and for me and for the children. You did far more than your share to pull us through.

I remember how we all needed you and how you always came through. I recall an experience we had while I worked for the Indian Seminary Department at Brigham City. I made a decision there about the time of day the Indian students should come to seminary. I felt that it was a sound and wise decision. My leaders in the head office felt that I had erred in judgment. They came to Brigham City and kindly criticized me. I wanted so much to be successful, to be known as a good teacher and a wise administrator. Feeling that my leaders had lost confidence in me pained my soul and caused me to doubt my own self-worth.

I didn't want to go home and tell you what had happened. I couldn't disappoint you. Yet I didn't know where else to go or whom else to tell. When I came home you were alone in the kitchen. The children were in the backyard.

I blurted out, "Marilyn, I've got some bad news." Then, with tear-filled eyes, I told you the story. When I finished I said, "So, Marilyn, my career is shot. I'm not going anywhere; you married a failure."

We looked deep into each other's eyes. You reached out and took my hand in yours and said, "George, I didn't marry a failure. Your career is not ruined. You are the greatest man that ever lived and I love you with all my heart."

Your voice was like the voice of an angel—all my doubts were swept away. I was a new man. I knew then what I've known so many times, that all that mattered to me was what you thought of me. Oh, how I needed you then and so many other times! You never have let me down—and what you have been to me you have also been to the children. You've carried your own heavy burden and yet you've had the strength to carry much of the load for each of us. Now, thinking back, I wonder how you did it. Strength that you scarcely could muster was needed to cook our meals, bathe the children, wipe their noses, change their diapers, read them books, sing them songs, help them with school work.

You didn't resent your duties, you only wanted me to understand that you were trying. You wanted to see in my eyes that I could appreciate what you did rather than criticize what time and sometimes energy would not allow you to do.

You only wanted me to take my turn with home duties. You knew that when I came home at night I had worked all day and was tired. You just wanted me to know that you had worked all day, too. Instead of criticizing the cluttered house, I should have pitched in to clean things up. You didn't want me to help grudgingly, but willingly and with understanding. You wanted me to cheerfully care for the children while you went visiting teaching, to evening Relief Society preparation meetings, or to your much-loved genealogy class. You never wanted to back out of your lot; you just wanted me to be supportive of the most difficult of all tasks—that of being a mother.

I tried to help, but still you were pretty well on your own. When we would talk—and as I said, we didn't do that enough—you would tell me of your frustrations and of your joys. I remember when you told me of certain Relief Society lessons that meant so much to you because they focused light on the purpose of life and the nobility of motherhood. Another time you told me of your discussions with a sister in the ward with whom you went visiting teaching. You loved her because her life-style was similar to yours. You wouldn't tell me the complete content of such discussions because you said that sometimes you told her of my inadequacies and she spoke in the same way of her husband. But then you added that most of the time the two of you took turns bragging about the marvelous men to whom you were married.

You told me of some of the women you knew who were really struggling, torn by the conflicts between gospel principles and the philosophies of the world. These women were, as Elijah said, "halting between two opinions"; they were not comfortable with what they learned at church, nor could they fully embrace the things they were hearing from other sources.

You tearfully explained to me how grateful you were to base your goals upon divine and never-changing truths. You testified to me that you knew that each of our children had come to us from God. You expressed your deep desire to influence your children to do good. As we talked I was impressed with the insights and strength that were growing in your soul and that seemed to be nourished by the difficulties you were facing. I was grateful that my children had you for their connection with heaven.

I remember saying to you, "I suppose Mom had her difficult years." "I'm sure she did," you replied, adding, "I believe many women do, especially those who want to be good mothers. Now, as the older children are raised and the youngest ones are getting alarmingly close to leaving home, the rewards completely outweigh the burdens. Now, at times, I'm so proud I can hardly refrain from running to the phone to call my sister Sharon to tell her what Matt, or Kathryn, or Devin, or Marinda, or one of the others has done. Even when I am called upon in church to speak, I want to spend the whole time talking about my family. And that is what I'd do, except you tell me not to."

Now whenever you speak of your family you beam and almost glow. Has it all been worth it—I mean, considering the difficult years and all? I can hear your proud reply, "What do you think?"

I remember recently when one of our married children came in the house and asked, "Mom, could you tend my children for an hour?" You replied, "I sure can't—I'm off to teach my calligraphy class." (You're the best calligrapher in all of Salt Lake, in my opinion.) You picked up your supplies and hurried out the door. Your most difficult years are behind you, and you are willing to let your daughter endure her difficult years because you know the rewards of motherhood.

The fact is, you want for your daughters what you had for yourself. That is, I suppose, the best answer to the question, "Would you, my dear Marilyn, do it all over again?"

Just for a Change

SUSAN NOYES ANDERSON

Just for a change I'd like to make
a change this Mother's Day—
I'd like to do the things that all
those mothering books say.
I'd like to give up yelling and
perfect the old "I" statement.
Not "Turn that racket down!" . . .
but "I'm in need of noise abatement."
Not "Talk back once more and you're toast!"
but—"I demand respect."
Not "Brush your teeth, or die!" . . .
"I fear your hygiene is suspect."
I'd like to be the kind of mom
who gets the kids to clean
(and they all end up having fun,
and no one thinks you're mean)!
I'd like to be the kind who gets
the dinner on the table,
and never has to set it, 'cause
her children are so able. . . .
And willing, oh, I'd like to be
the kind that makes them willing—
I'd write a how-to book, and
would I ever make a killing!
I'd sort of like to be the type
who's frugal as can be,
and manages her time so well

she's always home by three.
The kind whose kids are never spoiled
because they love to work,
who think a kid who asks his mom
for money is a jerk.
I'd really like to be that kind—
and, oh, just one more thing . . .
I'd like to be the kind who's never
freaked by anything.
The kind who always keeps her cool,
no matter what goes down.
The kind who can control her kids
with one look, or one frown.
(Or two looks or two frowns, or even
one big burst of words!)
I'd like to be the kind who looks
real hip, but not absurd.
In short, I'd like to be a mom
who's good as good can be.
The only problem is, how would
my children know it's me?

"Get Used to It"

KAREN J. ASHTON

Moments after my first baby's birth they placed her in my arms. As I touched her tiny fingers I laughed and cried at the same time. She was beautiful! She opened her eyes and looked, for the first time, at the mortal world she was now a part of. I was seeing a brand new world myself. I was looking through the eyes of a mother. The pathway of life ahead of me, which had seemed to contain so many choices moments ago, had suddenly straightened out. Someone else's life and well-being depended on me. There would be no skydiving lessons, speedboat racing, or any other high-risk adventures. I prayed I would be equal to the responsibility. I was determined to be the best mother, homemaker, housekeeper, hostess, Saint, and citizen the world had ever seen.

The windows of heaven opened over the next few years and it rained babies. By the time Emily was three we had two other children and a good case of reality had set in. There were dishes, diapers, earaches, doctors, errands, and meals. That doesn't begin to mention the weightier responsibilities of teaching my little ones the gospel and being a worthy example. Nothing I had ever heard or read had prepared me for the physical and emotional intensity of motherhood. Physically, there was no rest. I had a new sympathy for the little robin outside my window who was forever feeding and warming her young. Emotionally, huge roots of love had grown into and around my heart. I knew that if something were to hurt my children or suddenly take them from me I would bleed uncontrollably. I loved my children as I had never loved anything or anyone in my life. Even when I managed to get away, the anxiety for their well-being would thunder over me like a herd of elephants. Frankly, I was exhausted.

One morning, I called my mother and cried: "I'm so tired. I'm going to die!" Her reply was short and to the point. "Get used to it. You're going to feel that way the rest of your life." I was stunned by her blunt and seemingly uncaring remark. Later that day I happened to relate my mother's comment to another young mother. I couldn't believe it. She laughed! Then, to my surprise, I laughed too. Neither of us questioned the truth of what my mother had said. Somehow, laughing about it brought relief and broke the tension and fatigue I had been feeling all morning.

Because parenthood is the highest and holiest of callings, it's easy to feel overwhelmed with the responsibility and forget to enjoy the process. The Lord wants us to be happy and find joy in our work as well as joy in our posterity. Understanding God's love for us and for our children should fill us with hope, happiness, and good cheer.

The Red Silk Dress

ARDETH G. KAPP

While my husband, Heber, presided over the Canada Vancouver Mission, I was profoundly impressed by something I observed when he and I attended stake conferences in the far northern part of the province. During our three years in the mission we attended twice each year, making six conferences in all. Following that first conference, etched into my mind and heart was the memory of a young family sitting on the front row. They came from some distance to be there; they lived in the village of Horsefly, beyond One Hundred Mile House, in a very small branch of the Church. Mother and father, three older brothers, one older sister, and one young boy, about ten years of age, sang with enthusiasm, "We Thank Thee, O God, for a Prophet." It seemed as though they were a small chorus by themselves, all watching the chorister as if they had been trained, with the entire congregation accompanying them. One of the older boys stood holding the hymnbook in both hands, with his arms wrapped like parentheses around his younger brother standing in front of him.

During the conference, each member of the family appeared to be hanging on every word spoken, as if they had come with a bucket to be filled. Occasionally some interaction between an older brother and the younger boy revealed the closeness of their relationship.

The mother was wearing a red silk dress. But it was not the dress that initially caught my attention; it was her expression of joyful abundance as she leaned forward occasionally to look over her family, as if to be reassured of her wealth. Every child was in place, responsive to all that was going on.

Six months later, the same events were repeated, with only minor changes. Some of the family members wore new clothes to accommodate their growing years, but the mother was still attired in her red silk dress.

Over the course of three years, young men and women show signs of growth and change. And yet, some things remain the same. Each time we attended stake conference, we eagerly looked forward to seeing this family in their places on the front row. Each time, the faithful mother wore the same red silk dress. It always looked nice, almost new, as if it were simply resistant to wear. The dress was becoming a symbol to me of selfless sacrifice, eternal priorities, and an understanding of lasting values.

The last conference we were to attend with the Saints in that distant area, we anxiously anticipated what we had come to consider a vital part of the conference. I found myself hoping that the sermon that had become so vivid in my mind and heart each conference relating to humility, spirituality, and seeking first the kingdom of God would not be interrupted or lessened. I wanted to come home remembering always the unspoken sermon, the lesson I had learned at that stake conference. I looked anxiously for the mother in her red silk dress.

Finally the family arrived, taking their place on the front row. The eldest boy, now nineteen years of age, wore a new suit, white shirt, and tie. The younger brothers had new shirts and pants. Their sister's stylish, youthful dress was obviously a recent purchase; she wore it with a wonderful smile of satisfaction and joy. Mom and Dad were in their usual places, anchors to the family. There was the eldest son, prepared to leave for his mission. He was ready to launch out into the world of service to the Lord. His mother sat there in her red silk dress, her face reflecting her inexpressible joy. The sermon was complete, the message delivered, the events recorded.

Now, if that boy were asked after arriving in the mission field, "What comes to your mind when you think of your mom?" it is hard to imagine him saying, "She had one silk dress and wore it every Sunday." But it is very possible that what that dress symbolized will never be forgotten.

"*D*o You Think That
I Don't Love You?"

LaDAWN A. JACOB

Several years ago, a dear friend I will call Pam went through some tremendous trials. Her husband developed chemical allergies and was unable even to go out of the house. He stayed in a tiled room, and Pamela put his food outside the door and then told him on the intercom that it was ready. They had four sons and a baby daughter. Hoping for improvement, they decided to move from California to Arizona, which had fewer air pollutants. Finding a home and caring for her sick husband and her children was incredibly stressful. Pam also suffered a physical illness that caused all her hair to fall out. She had no eyelashes, no eyebrows, and was completely bald.

One day she was driving between the home where her husband was staying and the one where she was staying with their children (he couldn't be around anyone who had been contaminated with chemical pollutants). As she drove, she said, "I thought of all of the dreams of my life and how many had not come true as I thought that they would. A lot of those dreams had shattered and fallen down around me. I also thought as I drove along how ugly I was. Nobody could love me, I was so bald and thin and unattractive." As the tears began to flow, she felt a warmth around her and the words, "Do you think that I don't love you?" She remembered the love of the Savior for her. She knew she was precious to him. The warmth of that moment carried her through many, many weeks of difficult times.

God's nurturing can be felt in warm support as we learn to be nurturers, even when we are dealing with the pinpricks of daily life.

Mother Came First

GEORGE D. DURRANT

I recall coming home from my mission. There on the railroad platform was the girl I was going to marry, and near her was my mother. My girlfriend happened to be standing in a position where I got to her first. But I passed right by her and took my mother into my arms. If it hadn't been for my mother I'd never have been coming home from my mission, for she had taught me what I needed to know in order to be a missionary. It was she who had said she'd take care of the chicken farm while I was gone. She gathered eggs in the winter, summer, fall, and spring, in snowstorms, rainstorms, and hot summer; because my father was sick, and my mother knew that the only way I could stay on my mission was for her to support me financially.

So I made certain that my mother was the first to receive my greeting as I arrived home. Later, of course, there was time for the girlfriend.

The Choice

WILFORD WOODRUFF

December 3rd [1838] found my wife very low. I spent the day in taking care of her, and the following day I returned to Eaton [Ohio] to get some things for her. She seemed to be gradually sinking and in the evening her spirit apparently left her body, and she was dead.

The sisters gathered around her body, weeping, while I stood looking at her in sorrow. The spirit and power of God began to rest upon me until, for the first time during her sickness, faith filled my soul, although she lay before me as one dead.

I had some oil that was consecrated for my anointing while in Kirtland. I took it and consecrated it again before the Lord for anointing the sick. I then bowed down before the Lord and prayed for the life of my companion, and I anointed her body with the oil in the name of the Lord. I laid my hands upon her, and in the name of Jesus Christ I rebuked the power of death and the destroyer, and commanded the same to depart from her, and the spirit of life to enter her body.

Her spirit returned to her body, and from that hour she was made whole; and we all felt to praise the name of God, and to trust in Him and to keep His commandments.

While this operation was going on with me (as my wife related afterwards) her spirit left her body, and she saw it lying upon the bed, and the sisters weeping. She looked at them and at me, and upon her babe, and, while gazing upon this scene, two personages came into the room carrying a coffin and told her they had come for her body. One of these messengers informed her that she could have her choice: she might go to rest in the spirit world, or, on one condition she could have the privilege of returning to her tabernacle and continuing her labors upon the earth. The condition was, if she felt that she could stand by her husband, and with him pass through all the cares, trials, tribulation and afflictions of life which he would be called to pass through for the gospel's sake unto the end. When she looked at the situation of her husband and child she said: "Yes, I will do it!"

At the moment that decision was made the power of faith rested upon me, and when I administered unto her, her spirit entered her tabernacle, and she saw the messengers carry the coffin out at the door.

"$\mathcal{J}$s William Going?"

LEONARD J. ARRINGTON AND
SUSAN ARRINGTON MADSEN

Editor's Note: Drusilla Dorris of Tennessee married James Hendricks of Kentucky in 1827, and they became members of the Church in 1835. As the following account shows, Drusilla's was a life of courageous and faithful endurance in the midst of difficult trials.

Following their baptism in 1835, Drusilla Hendricks and her husband, James, were immediately rejected by members of their families. James's relatives forbade any family members to enter James and Drusilla's home, and relatives on both sides scorned them openly in their church meetings, praying for their souls which had surely "gone to the devil." Rocks were hurled at them and their home, and their property was frequently vandalized.

As soon as they were financially able, Drusilla and James began their journey to Clay County, Missouri, where the Saints were gathering. Drusilla recalled that as they left their home in Tennessee, "I had four sisters to leave but only one to regret our leaving. She was a Latter-day Saint." Drusilla had been very close to her sisters while growing up and until her baptism "we never met or parted without crying."

The move to Missouri, however, was to be only the first in a long series of moves they would be forced to make because of their religious beliefs. Within a short time, anti-Mormon mobs forced them to move from Clay to Caldwell County. It was during their stay there in 1838 that James suffered an injury that would cripple him for the rest of his life. Charles C. Rich called at the

Hendrickses' home late one night to summon James to assist the Mormons against a mob assembled on Crooked River, just a few miles south of where they were living. "Don't get shot in the back," Drusilla said to James as she handed him the gun. The next time she saw him, James was on a bed, a shot in the neck having paralyzed him from the neck down.

Through the moves from Missouri to Quincy, Illinois, to Nauvoo and on towards Winter Quarters, Nebraska, James improved, but nearly all of the responsibility for caring for the family and transporting them from place to place fell upon Drusilla. "I had to lift my husband at least fifty times a day and in doing so I had to strain every nerve," she records. One can imagine this young mother, with five children under the age of ten and a husband in very poor health, caring for her family's daily needs of food and clothing, as well as milking cows, feeding livestock, trying to grow a garden, maintaining their living quarters, and trying to bring in money for supplies by taking in boarders, washing, and sewing. In addition, she strained under the emotional pressure of being surrounded by anti-Mormon sentiment and persecution. . . .

Only Drusilla's oldest son, William, was of much help to his mother. One of her greatest trials was the call he received to join the ranks of the Mormon Battalion. Drusilla wrote how "one would say to me, Is William going? I answered, No he is not. Then another would ask, Is William going? No. Why, they said, they would not have their son or husband stay for anything. Then I would say, a burned child dreads the fire."

Then Drusilla recounts how when she was alone she had second thoughts: "The whispering of the Spirit would say to me: 'Are you afraid to trust the God of Israel? Has He not been with you in all your trials? Has He not provided for your wants?' Then I would have to acknowledge the hand of God in all His goodness to me."

The day of mustering-in dawned, finding Drusilla still adamant. She recorded how William set off for the morning chores:

"My eyes followed him as he started through the tall heavy grass wet with dew. I thought how easy something might happen, for that was a sickly climate. I got ready to get breakfast and when I stepped up on the wagon tongue to get my flour I was asked by the same spirit that had spoken to me before, if I did not want the greatest glory and I answered with my natural voice, Yes, I did. Then how can you get it without making the greatest sacrifices, said the voice. I answered Lord, what lack I yet? Let your son go in the Battalion, said the voice.

"I said, It is too late. They are to be marched off this morning. That spirit then left me with the heartache. I got breakfast and called the girls and their Father to come to the tent for prayers. William came— wet with dew from the grass and we sat down around the board and my husband commenced asking the blessing on the food. Then Thomas Williams came shouting at the top of his voice, saying 'Turn out men, turn out, for we do not wish to press you but we lack some men yet in the Battalion.' William raised his eyes and looked me in the face. I knew then that he would go as well as I know now that he has been. . . . I went to milk the cows. . . . I thought the cows would be shelter for me and I knelt down and told the Lord if He wanted my child to take him, only spare his life. . . . I felt it was all I could do. Then a voice . . . answered me saying, It shall be done unto you as it was unto Abraham when he offered Isaac on the altar. I don't know whether I milked or not for I felt the Lord had spoken to me."

Drusilla's earnest prayer was answered, for William survived the Battalion march and joined his family after they had arrived in the Salt Lake Valley. Together they went on to help settle Cache Valley. William later pioneered in southern Idaho and in Latter-day Saint colonies in northern Mexico.

Drusilla's husband, James, survived the crossing of the Great Plains and became the first bishop of the Salt Lake City Nineteenth Ward, while Drusilla served as Relief Society president. She continued to support her family as well as several grandchildren by taking in boarders and managing the old Warm Springs Bathhouse in northwest Salt Lake City. She wrote during her final years, "The gospel is true. I have rejoiced in it through all my trials for the Spirit of the Lord has buoyed me up or I should have failed."

$\mathscr{A}$ Drink of Water

ANNIE PIKE GREENWOOD

When I was a child and used to wake at night, fearing the engulfing dark I would call, "Mama! Mama! I want—a drink—of water!"

No matter how faint my voice, she always heard and gave answering presence, dispelling the strangeness of the shadowy room as she came. I see her yet, sweet angel, in her long white gown there in the moonlight, or softly luminous through the star-lit dark. No matter how tired, no matter how sick, she always came. And now I know that the thing which caused her death—cancer—was often stabbing under her heart even as she uncomplainingly held to my childish lips that drink of water. I wonder if she ever guessed that my thirst was really for her consoling presence? She brought me the drink of water—and she brought me more than that: love, and security, and peace. Yea, she brought more, even, than that.

When my first-born was about three years old he often woke me at night by his fretful cries for a drink of water. I was very tired, and it seemed to me that I would no sooner fall asleep than his little voice would rouse me with "Mama! Mama! I want—a drink—of water!" And more than once I spoke impatiently to him. I called him "Dearie," and "Sweetheart," but my voice was harshly impatient. I went back to bed and thought to return to sleep, but I found myself recalling the time when I, too, was a little child calling for water in the night, and I saw her (patient, lovely mother!) bending above me, the glass of water in her hand, breathing words of love. Had she answered my demand impatiently I would have cowered back into my little bed with sobs of despair. Oh, my little son!—that you should have had a mother so unworthy!—I slipped from the bed and went to look upon my darling's face. I remembered with a pang that he had whimpered when I told him to lie still and not bother me again. To what sad dreams had I sent the lonely little fellow by my impatient words? To whom on earth might he turn for that inopportune drink if not to his mother? I knelt beside him long with my arm about his little body. Oh, how I hope that the memory of that night will be blotted from his mind! But how can we tell what he will remember?

I shall never be the patient mother that she was, but I try not to murmur at the demands of my little ones even though I may be both tired and sick, for how can I tell at what moment is being impressed upon their minds the image of me which they will bear through life? How happy I would be if at some trying time in their lives they might be set upon the right path by remembering me, their mother, patiently and lovingly coming to them through the silent night with a drink of water.

On the
Lighter Side

ℐerfecting Motherhood

KATHLEEN "CASEY" NULL

W ell, mothers, are you weary of the well-doing mother you hear lauded from the pulpit every Mother's Day? Have you had it with the guilts?

Not to worry. You need not squirm through another Mother's Day program, or smile sheepishly when you are handed your annual carnation.

Those days are behind you. Yes, you too can be a perfect mother. And you can be perfect, beginning today. Or tomorrow. First of all you must get up three hours before your family does. On Sundays make it five hours. Use those hours to:

—Read your scriptures.
—Pray.
—Exercise.
—Shower or bathe and groom yourself (include full manicure, pedicure, make-up, and hair styling).
—Dress (delete sweat pants, T-shirts, jogging shoes—unless they are new and made of leather; include a freshly starched, lace-edged apron).
—Work in garden (bring a basket outside with you to fill with fresh fruit for breakfast and fresh flowers for the table).
—Prepare hot breakfast.
—Set table with china, crystal, and linen.
—Put home in order.
—Practice musical instrument.
—Wake up family.
—Make beds (check to be certain bed is unoccupied before

making; sometimes it is difficult for little ones to get out of a freshly made bed, especially if you use hospital corners).

It is now six o'clock A.M. Time for the family devotional. You will have taught your family to sing various choral arrangements by Handel. There will be at least two family members for each of six parts. Have your five-year-old read a chapter from the Book of Mormon. This will give you an opportunity to teach patience to your family, by example.

At eight A.M. you will leave the home in an immaculate condition (and that is an important point) with three preschoolers, and the baby in tow to:

—Buy groceries for three weeks.
—Go visiting teaching.
—Purchase fabric to make new covers for living room couch and love seat.
—Take your children to the pediatrician for their weekly checkup.
—Attend a community development meeting, at which you volunteer to chair the "Let's Clean Up Our City" committee.

You'll be home by nine-thirty and will have time to put away the groceries, make the couch and love seat covers, and play chess with your children before you eat a hot lunch together (you are teaching them table etiquette), and put them into their beds for a nap.

While they nap, you can wash eight loads of laundry, iron it, put it away, put up wallpaper in the dining room, harvest some vegetables from the garden for dinner, make a quilt, and wash the lunch dishes.

While dinner is cooking, you really must prepare a family home evening lesson with visual aids, a Mother Education lesson for Relief Society on Sunday, and make the beds again.

After dinner, the family can practice their parts on the Bach piece you are working on, while everyone washes the dishes.

At family home evening you could follow up the lesson with a lesson in oil painting, ballet, or fencing. Then the family can meet in the family room for dessert—crepes suzette or Baked Alaska which you made at one o'clock A.M. that morning.

Once the family is tucked in you'll need to stay up for five or six more hours. This will give you the opportunity to bake a loaf of bread for the sister who just had a baby, hem your daughter's skirt, crochet a cap and mittens for your son who is on a mission in Norway, mop the floor, color code the family's socks, weed the strawberries, bake cookies for your son's first-grade field trip, write in your journal, make granola for breakfast in the morning, and iron tomorrow's apron.

Try to get to bed before two o'clock A.M. After all, it will be a quarter of three before you know it, and time to begin another day.

On the other hand, maybe you'd rather settle for just being a *good* mother and get a little shut-eye.

$\mathcal{M}$ashed Potatoes

JANE F. HINCKLEY

Editor's Note: The following selection comes from a book about Marjorie Pay Hinckley, wife of Church President Gordon B. Hinckley. Jane F. Hinckley is a daughter-in-law to President and Sister Hinckley.

I must admit I fell in love with my future mother-in-law almost before I fell in love with her son Richard. I always knew that she would be the best mother-in-law a person could ever have. No one could have been better. She has never corrected me. She has never criticized me. She has always been so accepting.

One Sunday evening, early in our marriage, we were visiting Dick's parents. His mother wasn't feeling well and was lying down. We offered to fix dinner for the family. I peeled and mashed some red potatoes. After we served them to everyone, Dick said, "I don't think you're supposed to mash red potatoes." His mother quickly said, "Jane can mash any kind of potatoes she wants to mash! They're delicious."

That was typical. I have never felt judged. She has always expressed confidence in me and admiration for everything I do.

The Real "Facts of Life"

JANENE WOLSEY BAADSGAARD

I used to write a column for the *Deseret News* on family life. One week I asked my readers for ideas on how to reduce the costs involved in having children.

One response I received offered a rather blunt suggestion. The unsigned note read, "Try birth control pills, abstinence. You don't need to be so self-indulgent."

Well . . . I used to be naive enough to believe that kind of propaganda myself. But since I've become a parent, I've had my eyes opened to the real "facts of life."

The problem with this reader's fact-oriented advice is that it fails to tell the real truth about how babies get here to start with. Babies aren't caused by . . . well, you know. If it were as simple as that, then everybody who wanted a baby would have one and those who didn't want one would never have any surprises.

There are far more reliable rules for contraception than this sincere but misinformed reader had to offer. If you want to be sure you don't get in a delicate condition,

1. announce to your parents, in-laws, friends, neighbors, co-workers, and ward or branch members that you and your husband are going to start your family now.

2. spend your savings redecorating your study into a nursery.

3. promise your daughter a baby sister for Christmas.

4. buy a bigger house.

5. quit your well-paying job after announcing to the world you are anxious for motherhood before it's too late.

6. graduate with straight A's in child development, obtain a

master's degree in family relations and a Ph.D. in home management.

On the other hand, this is how babies are really made. Babies are made when

1. a wife finds a fascinating new career she loves, with unlimited possibilities for fame and fortune, and happily assures her new employer that she won't be having any more babies.

2. a husband and wife decide they have enough children and proceed to sell or give away all their baby clothes, furniture, and maternity clothes.

3. a doctor reassures a woman she doesn't need to worry any longer because she has "gone through the change."

4. a woman goes on a diet with her husband in which the first one to lose twenty pounds gets a whole new wardrobe.

5. the wife spends a seven-year clothing allowance on one dozen tight, form-fitting dresses.

6. a couple finally give up on the infertility doctors and decide to adopt triplets. This happy pair will promptly become pregnant with twins.

7. the couple forget to keep insurance policy payments current and find out they have been dropped from coverage, maternity benefits and all.

"Where Did She Come From?"

MICHAELENE P. GRASSLI

My friend Jan and her husband adopted a baby. When four-year-old Scott, a neighbor, came to visit, he looked at Jan, scrutinizing her carefully. Then he looked at the baby. Curious, he asked, "How did that baby get here? You didn't have a big tummy. Where did she come from?"

Not wanting to go into too much detail, Jan replied, "You're right, Scott. This baby didn't grow inside me, but Heavenly Father brought her just the same."

Scott's eyes got big in amazement. He sputtered, "You mean . . . you mean he was *right here* and you didn't call me!"

$\mathscr{G}$hostly Visitors

A. GAIL SMITH

$\mathbf{M}$ama had creative ways of expressing her wonderful sense of humor. Halloween was one outlet for such expression. Each Halloween, with great secrecy, she would plan and plot with us over how we would disguise ourselves to go about the town trick-or-treating.

It was a small town, so it was not difficult or time-consuming to cover the entire community, knocking on every door with a "Trick-or-Treat!" Some of the people would make us do a trick, such as reciting a poem or singing a song, to earn our treat.

The year I was ten, I went trick-or-treating with Uncle Kendyl, who, despite his exalted title, was my own age and also my good friend. We dressed up as farmers and managed to come up with the money to buy simple masks at Abner's Store. That night since we were in the middle of remodeling Great-grandmother Averett's house, I was to stay at my Granny Wilkins's house with Kendyl.

We returned after an hour of trick-or-treating, our bags bulging with treats, which we dumped out on the living-room floor. We were busy comparing candy, swapping items, and critiquing the contributions of the donors when we heard a knock on the door. I ran to get it as quickly as I could, knowing that it was probably more trick-or-treaters.

I was right, but the visitors weren't children. There in the doorway stood two huge ghosts. Aunt Nola Wilkins invited them in. As I stepped quickly aside, the two big ghosts floated in and sat down together on the piano bench, just in front of our piles of candy. I immediately went back to guard my candy and look up at those enormous ghosts. They had to be adults. Granny came in from the kitchen, wiping her wet hands on her apron.

"Who are you?" asked Aunt Nola.

The ghosts gave no answer.

"Do you live in this town?"

They nodded.

"Do we know you?"

Again a nod.

"Do you live close by?"

The ghosts shrugged.

Kendyl and I, intrigued, joined in the questioning, but the ghosts' identity remained a mystery. Then the ghost nearest me looked down and, behind the hole cut for its mouth, grimaced at me. I could see the teeth and part of the lips. My mind began to race. I had seen that grimace and those teeth before. But where? I searched my memory. Where, where?

Suddenly it came to me. I burst out, "I know you! I've seen those teeth before." The ghost chuckled and then I was absolutely sure. It was my mother. The other ghost was my Aunt Nola Cooper.

I think often of what it meant that my mother was willing to ruin two perfectly good sheets to step out of her workaday identity as Glenna Cooper for a few hours to mystify and delight us children. I hope I show the same imagination with my own children.

"*I* Don't Think I'll Get Married in the Temple"

BETTE S. MOLGARD

When my son McKay was about ten years old, he was fascinated by the Olympics. Every second he could watch the competition, he sat riveted to the television.

One day I sat down to watch the ceremony at which medals were being handed out. McKay watched intently, then turned and asked, "Mom, would you be proud of me if I got ten gold medals?"

Sensing a teaching moment, I replied, "Yes, I would be proud of you if you earned ten medals. But there are some things that you can do that would bring me more pride than Olympic glory ever would. Watching you serve a worthy mission and then come home and get married in the temple would be the best way you could make me pop my buttons."

He considered my answer, then responded, "I'm going to go on a mission, but I don't think I'll get married in the temple."

My heart dropped. After years of careful instruction, my son had already decided against a temple marriage. I carefully inquired, "Why won't you be getting married in the temple?"

He looked at me, wrinkled his nose, and explained, "I can't think of any girl I know that I'd want to spend eternity with."

Mother's Day Shouldn't Be Guilt Day

KATHLEEN "CASEY" NULL

For many of us, Mother's Day could just as easily be called National Guilt Day.

We sit in pews, hankies in hand. Our tears are for those wonderful mothers we hear about that we still emulate.

We look around us, for we are certain those other mothers in attendance are the ones who are the appropriate recipients of all that praise and adoration.

For me it began even before the birth of my first child. Only a few months along, I attended the traditional Sunday Mother's Day meetings, my dress straining under the pressure of expansion.

When the young men in the ward began to pass out the pink carnations, I began to be nudged.

"Stand up! Stand up!"

I didn't.

I couldn't.

I knew those tributes and flowers were not intended for me. And somehow I knew that next year I would, of course, be that mother they described and I would proudly stand and accept a carnation.

I continued to attend on succeeding Mother's Days, but I never could figure out who that mother was that was honored from the pulpit each year. I dutifully accepted my flower or booklet, my consolation prize.

After all, these tributes were presented on Sunday, and if my family and I were in attendance at all, even with mismatched socks and unruly cowlicks, I didn't get them there on time by singing lullabies and gently sponging apple cheeks.

Then I began to think of this wonderful mother as a symbol, not unlike the familiar, ageless, motherly baker whose face appears on all those boxes of cake mix. She's a masthead of maternity. A goal.

I would leave my meetings on those Sundays full of resolve. I must bake, sing, and speak softly much more . . .

But I never did.

And now Mother's Day is here again.

My son just handed me a card he made in school. It was flowery and sticky (literally). On the outside it says,

"I Love You, Mommy, because . . ."

Here it comes. The moment of truth. I opened the card.

". . . you like to ride on roller coasters."

You mean after all these years of thinking I must bake more cakes and trying to be a perfect mother, I never realized I could be a perfectly acceptable mother just by doing what I like to do anyway?

To perfectly acceptable mothers everywhere: Happy Mother's Day!

$\mathscr{A}$ Disarming Humor

KATHLEEN H. BARNES

Editor's Note: The following selection comes from a book about Marjorie Pay Hinckley, wife of Church President Gordon B. Hinckley. Kathleen H. Barnes is the oldest of President and Sister Hinckley's five children.

I always assumed that motherhood would be easy. As the oldest child, I had watched Mother welcome each subsequent new baby into our family. It appeared to me to be an occasion that was unequaled in this life. Mother's ease with her children led me to believe that all of motherhood was joy, bliss, and complete satisfaction. She would tell me that the experience of childbirth was akin to dipping into heaven for a brief moment and returning with this blessed new infant. She said that with each new baby came a bundle of love so love never ran thin. She told me that the greatest joys in life were those associated with your children. It appeared to be all true.

When our youngest sister was born, I was ecstatic. I would jump off the school bus each school afternoon and run all the way home, so anxious was I to get home to the new baby. I held her and dressed her and fed her and bathed her. I took her for walks, and when she fussed I handed her to Mother. I agreed with Mother. Having a baby of your own would be the best!

Is it any wonder, then, that my intense hunger for my own baby started immediately after I was married? I would often imagine my day with a baby in it. I would see myself holding a baby, dressing a baby, cooing to a baby, loving a baby. I could hardly wait till my dream came true. But, as that blessed state of impending motherhood descended upon me, I found myself sick! Very sick! I couldn't eat or even smell anything that resembled food. I couldn't wake up, and slept night and day. My head was continually in a fog. This was not the way I had pictured it.

The night this first little infant was born didn't exactly feel like a trip to heaven. It was long, miserable, and something I vowed I would never repeat. When she finally arrived, I thought the hard part was over and from this moment forward, the bliss part of motherhood would begin.

Wrong. I took the baby home, thinking the routine of my life would quickly be resumed. My fantasies of dressing her in bows and lace were just around the corner. She was so cute—in fact, she was beautiful. This was going to be great after all.

But I was ill prepared for what I faced. This tiny little six-pound bundle instantly took total control of my life. She determined when I could sleep, when I could eat, when I could shower, clean my house, do my laundry, where and if I could go anyplace. Not only that, everything I did was done in a state of complete fatigue. About six weeks into this I looked around one day and knew that this was not the life I planned. And suddenly I desperately wanted out. Motherhood was not all it was cracked up to be. I wanted my old life back. I could not bear the thought of living the rest of my life out of control, in a completely fatigued state. In a flood of tears I dialed my mother.

"I've had it!" I cried to my mother. "I'm not cut out to be a mother! I can't do this the rest of my life. This child has taken over. I'm not even a person anymore. I want my old life back!"

She listened quietly as I unloaded for several tearful minutes. Then, quite unexpectedly, she started to laugh. "Well, guess what, dear," she said through her laughter. "It's too late!"

Her upbeat, jovial response disarmed me. I was completely taken aback. She had managed with that simple, light quip to bring me back to earth. The fact that she found my tragic situation funny suddenly allowed me to step outside myself and see how pathetic I looked. It was a comical sight. And somehow her laughter let me know that she knew what this was like and that it wouldn't last forever.

On so many occasions since then, Mother's disarming humor has put things into perspective. She takes life seriously, but she doesn't take herself seriously.

What a gift!

"𝒜 Mother for All Seasons?"

JANENE WOLSEY BAADSGAARD

A middle-aged woman approached me after I had finished giving a talk to her Relief Society and asked, "I have two children at home, two in elementary school, two in junior high school, two in high school, one on a mission, and one married with kids of her own. What does that make me . . . a mother for all seasons?"

"Tired," I replied.

An Eternal
Perspective

Thinking of You

BERTHA A. KLEINMAN

To the mother whose arms have never pressed
A baby's head to her lonely breast,
To the mother whose lips have never sung
A lullaby in a baby's tongue,
To the mother whose prayers through time and space
Have seemed to fail at the Throne of Grace—

No plea, no prayer, no tears of thine
Are ever wasted in God's design,
For He who counteth the sparrow's fall
Eternal increase shall yield to all,
And the motherhood that is here denied
Shall yet be given and glorified!

"You're Like a Mother"

ARDETH G. KAPP

The stake president sent me to you. He said you'd under-stand since you don't have any children either." Her tone of voice revealed an attitude of resentment as she stood at my front door, and although we were strangers at that moment, I recognized that seeming resentment as the cover for a troubled and anguished heart. During the several hours that followed, her concerns were spilled out, baring her soul. Tears flowed freely while she spoke of blessings denied.

She came as a stranger, but a sharing of deeply personal concerns made us sisters; and I gave silent thanks for the inspiration of the stake president who directed this sensitive young woman to my door. Upon leaving she turned and there was a brief moment of silence as our eyes met, and then in a tone of gratitude she said, "The stake president was right. You do understand. Thank you."

As she drove away, I rejoiced in the blessing it is to be able to ease the burden of another, for I did understand. And as I watched her car turn the corner, I was reminded of the words of Elder Neal A. Maxwell:

"Every time we navigate safely on this great and narrow way there are other ships that are nearly lost or which are lost which can find their way because of our light." (Brigham Young University fireside address.)

My path to understanding had not always been one of light; in fact, on occasion there were mists of darkness. Yet such mists are also necessary elements of our existence. As Bruce C. Hafen once stated: "There are conditions of uncertainty, difficulty, temptations and insecurity—and yet, they are the very fabric that gives mortality its profound meaning. For only under such conditions is it possible for man to reach enough, search enough, and yearn enough for real growth of the spirit to be possible." (Bruce C. Hafen, then associate professor of law, Brigham Young University.) It *is* possible, and yet there were times over the past years when I really wondered.

A typical time of darkness was a Sunday morning some years ago. Sunday School was a time for rejoicing—except on Mother's Day. But this year I told myself it would be different.

The organ music was playing softly as the young girls moved quietly down the aisle, passing the small plants—begonias—along each row to the mothers left standing. This year I had vowed that I would be braver than all the years before, but as each of the mothers received her small tribute and the girls approached my row those old familiar feelings returned, and I wished I hadn't come to Sunday School—at least not on Mother's Day.

The little pots in silver wrapping were passed along each row until all the mothers were seated and then, as before, one more plant was passed. And once again I heard the usual whisper, "Go ahead, you deserve it. It's okay, we've got plenty," and then forcing the little plant into my tightened fist someone whispered, "You're like a mother!"

The meeting ended and my escape through the cultural hall and out the back door seemed blocked with numberless unidentifiable objects. I must not cry; I must set a good example, especially since my husband was in the chapel carrying out the responsibilities of his calling and showing such genuine concern for others, never thinking of himself. But how could I forget myself when the pounding in my ears *"You're like a mother"* seemed to mock the beating of my heart, as my hands resisted the weight of the little begonia.

This year was no different. I thought of the saying "time heals all things," but years were passing and there was no healing, only anguish and heartache. My mind flooded with too frequently asked questions: Were not my eternal companion and I commanded to multiply and replenish the earth and to have joy in our posterity? Was there to be no posterity? No joy?

My steps quickened as I hurried to the shelter of my home just a few blocks from the church. But even there the echo of loneliness was challenging as I tried to ignore the dinner table set with love and care but with only two plates. Another day and I would try again, harder.

Weeks later the doorbell rang and a little lad new to our neighborhood looked up with eager eyes, asking, "Can your kids come out and play?"

A coldness seemed to creep over me as I almost whispered, "I don't have any."

The child in a somewhat questioning tone asked, "Aren't you a mother?"

With a quick and somewhat abrupt response my voice cracked, "No, I'm not."

The little boy's eyes squinted, and with his head cocked to one side in the innocence of childhood, he asked the question that I had never dared to put into words. "If you're not a mother, what are you?"

Behind the closed door with my back against the wall my whole soul cried out, "Dear God, if I'm not a mother, what am I?" And again the searching question—what was the divine plan for my husband and me? What would the Lord have us do?

Several of our closest and dearest friends had adopted children, bringing the joy of parenthood into their lives. These precious children were not *like* their very own, they *were* their very own. Through the sealing power of the holy priesthood, they were sealed in an eternal family unit.

We, too, desired to adopt and continued to inquire of the Lord through prayer and fasting, striving to know if adoption was his will, seeking divine guidance as spoken of in the scriptures:

"But, behold, I say unto you, that you must study it out in your mind; then you must ask me if it be right, and if it is right I will cause that your bosom shall burn within you; therefore, you shall feel that it is right.

"But if it be not right you shall have no such feelings, but you shall have a stupor of thought." (D&C 9:8–9.)

But why the stupor of thought when we yearned so for that burning in the bosom that we had come to rely on through past years of experience, that quiet confirmation that gives assurance of the Lord's will? We struggled with the desire to experience increased faith, that we might receive a positive response to our desired decision, but in our minds we could hear the words: "Whatsoever ye ask the Father in my name it shall be given unto you, that is expedient for you; and if ye ask anything that is not expedient for you, it shall turn unto your condemnation." (D&C 88:64–65.)

Like a bird flying through turbulent winds, I experienced many highs and lows during the following years. Then, finally, perhaps because of a readiness to receive, like a divine echo the message came:

"Trust in the Lord with all thine heart; and lean not unto thine own understanding. In all thy ways acknowledge him, and he shall direct thy paths." (Proverbs 3:5–6.) The words were not new but the message came as an answer to a fervent prayer. "Trust in the Lord." Surely this was the key.

Almost with excitement thoughts came flooding to my mind. Faith in the Lord Jesus Christ—was this not the first principle of the gospel? Faith in a loving father, a divine purpose, an eternal plan. Faith that all things shall come to pass in the due time of the Lord.

I waited anxiously to share these feelings with my husband, Heber. I always waited up until he returned from his meetings, even on late nights, because that "sharing time" had become so special. A reservoir of limitless power from which to draw strength exists in a home where a faithful, obedient servant of the Lord endowed with the holy priesthood of God honors that priesthood and magnifies his calling. This night I would ask for another blessing at the hands of my eternal companion through whom God would speak, and with increased faith we would know God's will concerning us.

Heber had a way of sensing when I needed to talk, and when he arrived home he knew this was one of those times. As we shared our feelings, the quiet hours passed until only embers were left glowing in the fireplace. Having entered into the patriarchal order of celestial marriage, I was able to have a blessing pronounced upon me through the power and authority of the priesthood by the patriarch in our home.

A bridge between heaven and earth was spanned through priesthood channels; and never again would there be that seemingly unquenchable thirst, for we had partaken of "living waters." Guided by the inspiration of the Lord, together we found the direction that would become our purpose for life. We recalled the words of President David O. McKay as we remembered them—the noblest aim in life is to strive to make other lives happy. I listened to my righteous companion, ever drawing strength from his counsel: "You need not possess children to love them; loving is not synonymous with possessing and possessing is not necessarily loving. The world is filled with people to be loved, guided, taught, lifted, and inspired."

And finally, together we reread the words of the prophet Joseph Fielding Smith: "If any worthy person is denied in this life the blessings which so readily come to others, and yet lives faithfully and to the best of his or her ability in striving to keep the commandments of the Lord, then nothing will be lost to him. Such a person will be given all the blessings that can be given. The Lord will make up to him the fulness after this life is ended and the full life has come. The Lord will not overlook a single soul who is worthy, but will grant to him all that can be given which . . ." (*Doctrines of Salvation* 2:176–77.)

I didn't hear Heber's final words as he quietly closed the book, for my soul was at peace, with my head resting on his shoulder.

Things were never quite the same after that. From this source of strength came a quiet peace like the rising of the sun when the warmth of its rays moves upward until it encompasses the entire sky and there are no clouds of darkness in any direction.

This eternal union would be preserved and we would grow toward perfection together as we made a vow to trust in the Lord and his timing, knowing that "all that my Father hath shall be given unto him." (D&C 84:38.) There would still be questions but there would also be answers. "What should we do in the meantime?" and "what is the purpose of life?" were the questions I asked the patriarch in our home, who holds the keys to our eternal family unit. His answer: "The noblest aim in life is to strive to make other lives happy."

I cannot recall just when it happened, but our cookie jar was just not large enough to contain all the cookies that were dispensed from our door in one day. And so it became a cookie drawer, familiar to the entire neighborhood, young and old. Even the priests would come, using the excuse "we need a cookie," hoping Heber would be home and would have time to listen to them, to have fun, to "throw in" a little "fatherly advice," as they called it.

My rewards for waiting came at many unexpected times, like at the grocery store when the boy bagging my groceries said very spontaneously as he tossed in the last item, "Your husband is a great guy to talk to."

And the letter to Heber from a grateful mother: "Thanks for talking to my boy; it has made all the difference. It's hard without a dad, but now he's decided he wants to go on a mission. Thank you for the time you spend with my son."

One day a little boy brushed past me at the kitchen door, coached by his friend who led the way. "Bradley sez ya get one in both hands" was the comment as his more experienced companion eagerly pulled the cookie drawer wide open to better choose. With a concealed smile I responded, "Bradley's right," as I observed their careful selection. Once made, the little scavengers bounded from the door with their treasure, and as I stood watching, my heart rejoiced.

A small miracle was beginning to take place. "I give unto men weakness that they may be humble; and my grace is sufficient for all men that humble themselves before me; for if they humble themselves before me, and have faith in me, then will I make weak things become strong unto them." (Ether 12:27.) An eternal union strengthened through seeming adversity and disappointment can be the foundation for eternal bonds of love, binding a companionship against all the threatening powers that beset the lives of mortals.

Blessings seemingly denied are often just delayed and only in matters of great consequence do souls become closely bound together as they reach upward to God. And he is there: "Lo, I am with you alway, even unto the end of the world." (Matthew 28:20.)

Years passed swiftly, bringing fulfillment of carefully laid plans as we shared the joy of seeing the sons and daughters of our friends leave for missions and plan for temple marriages. We even eventually shared that special excitement reserved only for "expectant" grandparents. While Heber became a power of unwavering strength, on occasion I would experience a fleeting yearning that would each time be quietly softened. At one such time a kind Father in heaven who knows and understands all things put into the mouth of one of his appointed servants during a setting apart blessing those words that would reconfirm and bring to our hearts that "peace that passeth all understanding." "Your desires are known, your Father in heaven is pleased with your patience, and every righteous desire will be fulfilled in his due time."

Through the years we have been blessed with boundless opportunities for growth and development—opportunities to serve our fellowmen, young and old, and to rejoice in the gift of life. We have been able to see God's handiwork in all that is good, to love deeply and grow spiritually, and "to strive to make other lives happy."

During the week following one Mother's Day, when sorting through the mail, I recognized the California return address and rejoiced in another letter from "one of my girls." Such letters usually came with the announcement of an important event, maybe a new little baby. But the message was different this time, like the answer to a long forgotten prayer:

"I would like to share with you some of the feelings I have at this Mother's Day time. When I was a small girl I can remember other Mother's Days—the passing out of carnations to the mothers in the ward and how special it seemed. Someday I could stand too, perhaps, and be honored along with the rest. This Mother's Day came with special meaning to me as my mind reflected back on a sweet, but frail, 96-year-old grandmother, the sacrifices and love of my own mother, a sweet mother-in-law who always listens, and now my own tiny, special daughter smiling trustingly at her awkward mother's handling.

"But not only did my thoughts reflect back to mothers of blood but to a special, beautiful person who so touched my life as to make me always love and respect her as certainly a mother to me in all the special qualities that go with the word. If you could only know the number of times just thinking of you softened a sometimes hardened heart or helped me to my knees when our Heavenly Father's guidance was so needed."

My heart was full to overflowing as my eyes filled with tears of gratitude and so blurred my vision that I could read no further. As the tears quietly rolled down my cheeks, I thought of the privilege that had been ours to touch in a meaningful way the lives of Jim, Karen, Becky, Paul, Mark, Mindy, Wanda, and the many other precious souls we have loved so deeply. And then I reflected on the many lives even yet to be reached and taught, loved and guided, and a silent prayer escaped my lips. "Thank you, dear God. Truly my cup runneth over. Thou hast allowed thy humble servants to be used as instruments in thy hands." "Be it unto me according to thy word." (Luke 1:38.)

With the tears brushed away, I continued reading:

"I love you so very much and I pray often that the Lord's guiding spirit may always be with you so that you can continue to bless the lives of those around you.

"You're like a mother to me. Love, Cathie."

A Change in Routine

KATHLEEN "CASEY" NULL

A change in routine. That's what I thought I needed.

And I got it, and then some. But it wasn't quite what I had had in mind.

Within a little over a week

- My car broke down—water pump.
- I developed an allergy to my contact lens solutions.
- I came down with strep throat, and it felt like hot coals when I tried to swallow. I quit using the phone when a friend thought I was a crank caller and hung up on me.
- The optometrist took away my lenses and left me in a blur.
- The plumbing backed up and flooded three carpeted rooms and my side of the closet.
- I broke out in hives from the antibiotics I was taking for strep throat.
- I came down with a sniffly virus.
- The doctor put me on a powerful antihistamine, and I developed a tendency to fall asleep in the middle of the day in the middle of the activities of four children.

So there I was, splotchy, itchy, car-less, drugged senseless, sniffly, blind, and trying to cope in a swampland.

Pathos was not my idea of a change in routine.

I sank into the couch feeling helplessly resigned to my fate, and my three-year-old, normally preoccupied with his needs, came and stroked my hair. "It's all right, Mommy, I'll take care of you," he said soothingly.

He brought me one of his blankets and a book. He tucked the blanket around me and handed me the book to read to him.

It was a child's book about the universe. We spent a quiet period lost in the solar system, marvelling over the way it was organized and ordered for us. My voice began to get a little choked up.

There wasn't anything on those pages that I didn't already know from somewhere, but I was overwhelmed at the beauty and awesomeness of it all and at him who organized it so precisely. My son looked up at me and patted my splotchy cheek. "It's all right, Mom."

Yes, it certainly is.

David

UDORA MORRIS

A sunbeam quickly flashes through the sky
And then is gone.
The world a lighter place, the day
A brighter day.
For it was here.

A soul makes earth a visit brief
And then returns.
Pain a little sharper, awareness greater still,
And love.
For he was here.

$\mathscr{A}$ Family Is . . .

ELAINE CANNON

Years ago Allen Beck started something when he wrote two charming pieces called "What Is a Boy?" and "What Is a Girl?" Today we'll take a look at what a family is—with apologies to Mr. Beck.

A family is God's way of blessing the world.

A family keeps a mother from doing the things she's always wanted to do until she is too old to do them. But somewhere along the way a family weaves such a magic that one day mother realizes that this, after all, is what she wanted to do all along. (As for fathers—they have to shave every day.)

Families are always multiplied by two and come in a wide range of mathematical combinations. This unique variety pack comes in assorted sizes, shapes, colors, dispositions, and bank accounts. Each additional member to the unit challenges, for a time, the lofty premise that all men are created equal—that newcomer gets more attention per hour than everyone else put together.

As we look at the individual components, it is easy to see what makes families exactly the way they are. From the youngest to the eldest, each member has a part to play.

The youngest member of the circle is termed the baby. This has nothing to do with age, actually, but rather a stage of being; for whether six months or sixty years old, the youngest child is persistently referred to as "the baby."

Babies are for picking—picking at, picking up, and picking up after. Babies are also for kissing and caring and diapering and for bedding and bottling, for holding and hugging.

They come equipped with an amazing gift for melting the most rugged father into a reasonable facsimile of jelly and convincing a mother that she'd rather have her hands in detergent than suntan oil any day.

Babies cause parents to love each other more deeply, to smile more through tears, to buy more film, lose more sleep, stay home from more parties, and become more painful bores. But they also remind them that heaven is really very close after all.

Yes, babies are for loving.

The next age group in the family is the toddlers. These little destroying angels may be found wherever there is water. They are also known to slide down the best furniture, sneeze when fed, and move restlessly from room to room leaving their trail behind them. The only time they are quiet is when they are doing something they shouldn't. Toddlers have a disarming way of charming. They smile their sweetest smile when they are about to be disciplined.

Toddlers are on the threshold of a great new world of learning. So toddlers are for teaching—teaching to sing, to pray, to read, to eat with forks instead of fingers, to understand that training pants are the road to freedom, to know right from wrong, and to recognize the difference between Jesus and Santa Claus. One of the nicest things about a toddler is that he loves you unabashedly, anyway.

Oh, toddlers are for loving.

Then there is that delightful stage when offspring can now advance to the nearest grade school. Grade-schoolers are famous for giggles and gum, for the blank spaces in the front of their smiles, for freckles sprinkled generously across the bridge of the nose, and for telling family secrets to neighbors.

They have a talent for running—running noses, running away, and running errands, and for running the bathroom water the longest with the least to show for it. They are for getting—measles at Christmas, and into trouble when you aren't looking. They are skilled at getting things into drawers already too full, and other things out of closets that shouldn't have been opened in the first place. They ask more questions and eat more times a day than you had in mind. They are just great at losing boots, sweaters, one glove, balls, books, lunch pails, and instructions. They are devoted to creatures of the earth that growl, slither, wiggle, or crawl. Grade-schoolers have been known to collect bottles, rocks, wrappers, and a fan club made up of proud parents and grandparents, of teachers and big sisters, especially when they perform in the school program.

Oh, grade-schoolers are for loving.

Teenagers in the family grow too much too soon, or too little too late. They make us proud with their beauty of body, quickness of wit, fierce loyalties, and the fact that they remembered our birthday with an extravagant gift without being told.

They are the challenge and the challenger. They challenge our authority, our decisions, our life-style, our system, our taste in music, and our turn to have the car.

They emerge smarter, stronger, and more spiritual than we. But let us remember that we lifted—dragged, fought, loved?—them to where they are today. We just won't talk about it in front of them—it would ruin the whole thing.

Yes, families are God's way of blessing the world, of shaping a strong, stubborn man into a strong, sensitive father, and a beautiful, bossy woman into a beautiful, blessed mother.

Families are for loving each other anyway. Yes, a family is God's way of blessing the world. Oh, thank God, families are forever!

The Inevitable Evolution

CAROLYN SESSIONS ALLEN

Grandmothers get younger every year. This observation seemed particularly apparent (at least to me) on the eve of my own grandmotherhood.

Once our oldest daughter married, an adjustment in itself, my husband and I began preparing for the next step in life's progression. Looking for a way to postpone appearing older, I considered telling our friends we had adopted our twenty-two-year-old daughter at the age of ten. But she looks so much like her dad, no one would believe us.

It didn't surprise us when the announcement of impending grandparenthood came wrapped as a Christmas present the following year. Receiving a customized "grandmother-to-be" card from my husband on Mother's Day caused more apprehension. Of course I retaliated on Father's Day.

Then came the shock of seeing "our little girl" pregnant! Because we live in another state, we hadn't been able to grow into the idea. At the time of the initial declaration of pregnancy, she was still skinny. We didn't see her again until she was seven months along. The words of a familiar song played in my head, *"Is this the little girl I carried? . . ."*

Somehow we made the drastic mistake of predicting that the baby would be born early. "Someone" had read "somewhere" that short women deliver early. Since our daughter is five foot one, we felt reasonably sure she qualified. Finally the call came, appropriately on Labor Day, and *only* ten days late!

Boarding a plane the next day, I suddenly noticed all the *real* grandmotherly and grandfatherly people around me. Sweet-faced, white-haired, bespectacled men and women filled the plane. I glanced in a mirror to see if I had unknowingly undergone a transformation to fit the image of my new status.

Reassured, I put the mirror back in my purse. After all, I still had young children at home. I monitored my diet and hair color. I exercised every day—if allowed to count running up and down the stairs dozens of times in the course of a normal day's activities. As I glanced around the plane, I wished I wore a sign declaring "I'm a Grandmother!" Certainly that would have surprised my co-passengers—maybe?

As the engines of the plane revved, my thoughts followed suit. *How will it feel to hold that first grandchild,* I anticipated, *an extension of myself reaching forward into the next generation?*

While the plane taxied and waited for takeoff, I wrote in my journal: "From where I'm seated, I cannot see out of the plane. I feel as if I'm flying into the unknown—and that's just how I feel about grandmotherhood. I'm taking off into a big unknown.

"What I *can* see is that this inevitable evolution is another precious link in the chain of eternity."

A Promise for Eternity

SUSAN NOYES ANDERSON

I think somehow
that long ago
in the eternities,
I was a special friend to you
and you a friend to me.

We shared a bond,
an understanding
that was quick and sure.
I wonder if we knew that it
would deepen and endure.

The tie between us
had to be
a very special kind—
for even in this earthly life
our paths have intertwined.

We were sisters,
bound by a love
so meaningful and rare,
that we must have had an inkling
of the destiny we'd share.

And once prepared
to leave the heavenly
sphere we'd always known,
surely we joined hands and vowed
to help each other home.

Now that we find ourselves
mother and daughter
on this earth,
please don't forget the vow we made
and its eternal worth.

For though I know
that in this life
the burden rests with me,
the promise we two sisters made
was for eternity.

$\mathscr{A}$ Very Special Mission

CAROLE KIRK

On September 14, 1994, as I returned to work from lunch, someone from security asked to see me. She directed me to a small interview room where I could see two of my friends in the doorway. As I stepped into the room, I saw two officers from the sheriff's department. They asked if I had a son named Scott. I answered that I did. They told me there had been an accident and that he hadn't made it.

My entire body began to tremble; I couldn't believe what I had just been told. I sobbed uncontrollably. This just couldn't be true. They sent for my son John Jr., who also worked in the building. The officers told me my daughter, Heather, was at home and was the first to know of Scott's death. I immediately tried to call her, but the line was busy. They said another officer was on his way to inform my husband, John.

Scott was twenty-one years old, and for the past several years had not lived as we had tried to teach him. I spent more sleepless nights than I care to remember pacing the living room floor, pleading with the Lord to return him home safely. We often fought, and I knew something had to change. I took a picture of him taken when he was two years old with me to work to remind me that there was a time I adored him. I'd remember passing his room and seeing that sweet little boy on his knees saying his prayers.

A couple of years before, I had heard several talks and read an article on the blessings of regular temple attendance. If there was ever anyone who needed blessings, it was me. I had determined that I would go to the temple once a week. With five children and a full-time job, I had not been to the temple the last several years unless it was to attend a marriage. The change was gradual, but Scott and I started talking. Even though he wasn't doing all he should, I was loving him again.

After about a year, Scott came to me and said, "I know you probably won't believe me, Mom, but I want to go on a mission, and I need you and Dad to support me if I'm going to make it." I was flabbergasted and overjoyed! He met with the bishop weekly. We began reading the Book of Mormon every night after dinner. He was called to teach the Blazers in Primary. It was truly a miracle.

As I drove home, I felt confused, lost, and sad beyond description. I thought of Doctrine and Covenants 122 where it says, "All these things shall give thee experience, and shall be for thy good. The Son of Man hath descended below them all. Art thou greater than he?" I prayed for the strength to get through the days ahead. I prayed that I wouldn't become bitter or blame God. I prayed that I wouldn't lose my testimony. I thought, *This is not what is supposed to be happening; something has gone terribly wrong.* Scott had just been made an elder and received his patriarchal blessing three weeks before. He was planning to go on his mission in January. Immediately the thought came into my mind—*He is on a mission. It's just going to be longer than you planned and to a place you hadn't dreamed of.* I can't describe the feeling of peace that came over me. In the midst of this terrible thing, I found myself feeling blessed that my son had been called on a very special mission. The Spirit whispered to my mind that Scott was at peace, that he was okay.

In the days that followed his death, I was overwhelmed by the love and concern expressed by our dear ward members, family, and friends. There was a steady stream of visitors and phone calls for three solid days. I was exhausted physically and emotionally, but I felt as though the Savior had wrapped us in his arms and was expressing his love for us through each person who came to our house or called on the phone. As I knelt in prayer, I found it strange that I was thanking the Lord for the many blessings that were coming to us as a result of Scott's death. His funeral was his missionary farewell. It was a deeply spiritual experience for each of us.

I have been active in the Church all my life and have always had a testimony. But life has so much more meaning now. I cherish each member of my family more, as well as my temple marriage and the promised blessings that accompany it. I have learned to love the Holy Ghost and to know why he is called the Comforter. He has taught me and comforted me more than I am able to express. In the temple several weeks after Scott's death, the Holy Ghost whispered to my mind that Scott was happier and working harder than ever before. He was preaching the gospel! What more could a mother hope for?

I have always known intellectually that the Savior loves us and knows us individually. Now I know, in a very personal way, that he loves me and knows me by name. He knows my pain and understands the longings of my soul. I learned that we all need quiet time in our lives because this is when the Spirit teaches and communicates with our souls. I have experienced the great blessings that come from regular temple attendance, daily scripture study, and trying to keep the commandments. I pray that I will be able to endure to the end, and look forward to the day when I can throw my arms around my beautiful son and hear all about his missionary experiences.

Celestial Love

BROOKIE PETERSON

There is a couple whose story is touching and tender. They are named Steve and Kathy. When Steve was young he always showed empathy for any boy who had been picked on or teased—he reached out to him and made him feel a part of the group by accepting him and standing up for him. Kathy too showed very early in life what a warm heart she had; she cared for those who suffered; she brought home and took care of crippled animals; and she had a special tenderness for children who were mistreated.

This young couple learned soon after they married that they were unlikely to have children of their own. So they adopted a child when they had been married only six months. Subsequently they did have born to them a son and a daughter. However, after these two children came Steve and Kathy were told that there would be no more natural children for them. They knew that adoption of normal children, with three already, was most unlikely.

They began to consider accepting exceptional or handicapped children into their family. Eventually they adopted five more children—four with Down's syndrome and one who was paralyzed. You can imagine that it was all they could do to keep up with their children's tremendous needs—both physical and financial. A few years after the adoption of their last child, Steve and Kathy, with the help of their extended family, were able to arrange for the temple sealing of all of these children to them.

Of course the three older children, now all teenagers, were to be part of this significant event. One Thursday morning in

February all ten of them came to the temple. The handicapped children needed a lot of help, and the older children provided it. The couple dressed in white and went to the sealing room. When all was in readiness the eight children were brought to the door; the workers and teenagers assisted the younger children. The door opened and into the room and to the altar came the children, all dressed in white.

When the whole family was gathered at that altar there was not a dry eye in the room. It was a beautiful sight and the consummation of the hope this couple had extended to their children—the sacrifices they had made, the training they had provided, but most especially the selfless love they had felt and exhibited. In the warmth of that love these children would be able to reach their greatest potential, which I felt would be to influence others to practice more love and better live the second great commandment. Surely those who participated in or witnessed that sealing caught an inspiring glimpse of celestial love.

The Bridge Through the Mist

KATHLEEN "CASEY" NULL

Here we stand on the edge
of the bridge.

We nod to acquaintances
and clutch our little ones.

And see the bobbing heads of humanity
stretching all the way to the mist.

We cannot see beyond the mist,
and are tearful when
a loved one disappears from our sight
and fearful as we near it.

What will become of us?
Does the bridge end?
Do we drop off the edge
into icy rapids
never to be seen again?

Do we dissolve into mist?
What becomes of us, all of us,
as we walk along?

"It goes on!" someone whispers.
"I know because I saw
beyond the mist.

I saw my grandmother
and her grandmother too.

They were walking together.
The destination lies beyond the mist."

"Can it be true?" whispers a hopeful voice.

"Let's join hands," whispers another.

Sister to sister, brother to brother,
father to son, mother to daughter,
husband to wife—

We join hands that cross the bridge through the mist,
Into eternity.

_/_ources and _𝒫_ermissions

Motherhood: A Divine Role

"'It Never Gets Better Than This'" by Ardeth G. Kapp, from _What Latter-day Stripling Warriors Learn from Their Mothers_ (Salt Lake City: Deseret Book Co., 1996), pp. 4–11.

"To Mother" by Elaine Cannon, from _Mothering_ (Salt Lake City: Bookcraft, 1993), pp. 24–25.

"If This Is the Best Time, I Don't Want to Be Around for the Worst" by Janene Wolsey Baadsgaard, from _Why Does My Mother's Day Potted Plant Always Die?_ (Salt Lake City: Deseret Book Co., 1988), pp. 3–5.

"From a New Mother" by Jeanette B. Jarvis, _Improvement Era,_ May 1952, p. 308.

"'Therefore He Made Mothers'" by Harold B. Lee, from _The Teachings of Harold B. Lee,_ ed. Clyde J. Williams (Salt Lake City: Bookcraft, 1996), pp. 290–91.

"Happy Mother's Day, Sweetheart" by Eileen Gibbons, _Improvement Era,_ May 1955, p. 328.

"A Parent's Reverie" by Susan Noyes Anderson, © 1996 by Susan D. (Noyes) Anderson, from _At the End of Your Rope, There's Hope: Parenting Teens in Crisis_ (Salt Lake City: Deseret Book Co., 1997), p. 140.

"The Issue Was Simple" by Patricia T. Holland, from Jeffrey R.

Holland and Patricia T. Holland, *On Earth As It Is in Heaven* (Salt Lake City: Deseret Book Co., 1989), p. 58.

"'Where Is My Mothers' Manual?'" by LaDawn A. Jacob, from "Strengthening Our Nurturing Natures," in *Every Good Thing: Talks from the 1997 BYU Women's Conference,* ed. Dawn Hall Anderson, Susette Fletcher Green, and Dlora Hall Dalton (Salt Lake City: Deseret Book Co., 1998), p. 174.

A Mother's Love

"Mother" by Joseph F. Smith, from "Mother," *Improvement Era,* May 1913, pp. 729–30.

"Thoughts Inspired by a Letter from a Daughter to a Mother" by S. Dilworth Young, from the compilation *LDS Women's Treasury: Insights and Inspiration for Today's Woman* (Salt Lake City: Deseret Book Co., 1997), p. 237.

"The Journal" by Elaine Cannon, from *Life—One to a Customer* (Salt Lake City: Bookcraft, 1981), pp. 44–45.

"To My Son" by Kaye R. Anderson. Previously unpublished.

"Just What He Needed" by Brookie Peterson, from *A Woman's Hope* (Salt Lake City: Bookcraft, 1991), p. 36.

"Why Does My Mother's Day Potted Plant Always Die?" by Janene Wolsey Baadsgaard, from *Why Does My Mother's Day Potted Plant Always Die?* (Salt Lake City: Deseret Book Co., 1988), pp. 53–56.

"Mrs. Harrison" by Glenn I. Latham, from *What's a Parent to Do? Solving Family Problems in a Christlike Way* (Salt Lake City: Deseret Book Co., 1997), p. 168.

"A Homemade Sissy" by George D. Durrant, from *Mother, Our Heavenly Connection* (Salt Lake City: Bookcraft, 1984), pp. 19–28.

"A Name That Began with *M*" by Elaine Cannon, from *Mothering* (Salt Lake City: Bookcraft, 1993), pp. 42–43.

"To My Mother" by Elise Richins. Previously unpublished.

"Who Has Held the Christ Child?" by Oscar W. McConkie, from Bruce R. McConkie, "Charity Which Never Faileth," *Relief Society Magazine*, March 1970, p. 169.

A Mother's Faith

"'Isn't That an Honor for Me?'" by Elaine Cannon, from *Life—One to a Customer* (Salt Lake City: Bookcraft, 1981), p. 130.

"When We Understand the Plan" by Edgar A. Guest, from *When Day Is Done* (Chicago: The Reilly and Lee Co., 1921), pp. 174–75.

"For the Love of My Mother" by Heber J. Grant, from "For the Love of My Mother," *Improvement Era*, May 1942, p. 271.

"'Who Was Praying for You?'" by Anita R. Canfield, from *Remember, and Perish Not* (Salt Lake City: Bookcraft, 1998), pp. 63–64.

"A Mother's Faith" by Marion D. Hanks, from *Bread Upon the Waters* (Salt Lake City: Bookcraft, 1991), pp. 148–49.

"The Consecrated Son" by Barbara B. Smith, from *A Fruitful Season* (Salt Lake City: Bookcraft, 1988), pp. 170–72.

"Mary Fielding Smith and the Power of Prayer" by Joseph Fielding Smith, from *Life of Joseph F. Smith* (Salt Lake City: Deseret News Press, 1938), pp. 130–33.

"A Bright Red Shawl" by Camilla Woodbury Judd, from "The Parker Family," in *Treasures of Pioneer History,* comp. Kate B. Carter, 6 vols. (Salt Lake City: Daughters of Utah Pioneers, 1952–57), 5:240–41.

"Act of Faith" by Marilynne Todd Linford, from *Give Mom a Standing Ovation* (Salt Lake City: Bookcraft, 1996), pp. 152–54.

"It Was His Duty" by Anita R. Canfield, from *By Small and Simple Things* (Salt Lake City: Bookcraft, 1999), pp. 15–18.

"An Unfinished Woman" by Jaroldeen Asplund Edwards, from *Celebration! Ten Principles of More Joyous Living* (Salt Lake City: Deseret Book Co., 1995), pp. 35–36.

"'Leave It Alone'" by Marilynne Todd Linford, from *Give Mom a Standing Ovation* (Salt Lake City: Bookcraft, 1996), pp. 86–87.

A Mother's Influence

"Singing Lessons" by Max and Bette Molgard, from *The Lord Looketh on the Heart* (Salt Lake City: Bookcraft, 1998), pp. 13–16.

"The Educated Parent" by Kathleen "Casey" Null, from "The Educated Parent," in Elaine Cannon, *As a Woman Thinketh* (Salt Lake City: Bookcraft, 1990), pp. 109–11, 117.

"The Record of Her Labors" by Ardeth G. Kapp, from *My Neighbor, My Sister, My Friend* (Salt Lake City: Deseret Book Co., 1990), pp. 129–31.

"She Taught Me to Pray" by George Albert Smith, from *The Teachings of George Albert Smith,* ed. Robert and Susan McIntosh (Salt Lake City: Bookcraft, 1996), pp. 114–15.

"The Reading Mother" by Strickland Gillilan, from *The Best Loved Poems of the American People,* sel. Hazel Felleman (New York: Doubleday, 1936), p. 376.

"Andy's Talk" by Michaelene P. Grassli, from *What I Have Learned from Children* (Salt Lake City: Deseret Book Co., 1993), pp. 68–69.

"Always" by Carolyn Sessions Allen, from Kathleen "Casey" Null and Carolyn Sessions Allen, *From Here to Maternity* (Salt Lake City: Bookcraft, 1987), pp. 94–95.

"'Mom Says I Shouldn't Go'" by George D. Durrant, from *The Art of Raising Parents: A Young Person's Guide* (Salt Lake City: Bookcraft, 1977), pp. 81–83.

"A Little Parable for Mothers" by Temple Bailey, from the lesson manual *A Book of Remembrance* (Salt Lake City: Genealogical Society of Utah, 1936), pp. 38–39.

Teaching Moments

"'You're Lucky Too'" by Joyce Erickson, from Bruce and Joyce Erickson, *When Life Doesn't Seem Fair* (Salt Lake City: Bookcraft, 1995), pp. 288–90. Used by permission.

"'Good Breathing, Son!'" by Glenn I. Latham, from *What's a Parent to Do? Solving Family Problems in a Christlike Way* (Salt Lake City: Deseret Book Co., 1997), pp. 53–54.

"The Bicycle Lesson" by Ardeth G. Kapp, from *My Neighbor, My Sister, My Friend* (Salt Lake City: Deseret Book Co., 1990), pp. 132–33.

"Preparing a Heart for the Spirit's Touch" by James M. Harper, from "Rearing Good Parents," in *Every Good Thing: Talks from the 1997 BYU Women's Conference,* ed. Dawn Hall Anderson, Susette Fletcher Green, and Dlora Hall Dalton (Salt Lake City: Deseret Book Co., 1998), p. 163.

"What Else Would He Forget?" by Anita R. Canfield, from *Remember, and Perish Not* (Salt Lake City: Bookcraft, 1998), pp. 72–73.

"An Easy Unconditionality" by Virginia H. Pearce, from Virginia H. Pearce, ed., *Glimpses into the Life and Heart of Marjorie Pay Hinckley* (Salt Lake City: Deseret Book Co., 1999), pp. 145–46.

"'I Don't Know If I Have a Testimony'" by Michaelene P. Grassli, from *What I Have Learned from Children* (Salt Lake City: Deseret Book Co., 1993), pp. 29–30.

"'Now I Can Shake Hands with the Priesthood of God'" by Matthew Cowley, from *Matthew Cowley Speaks* (Salt Lake City: Deseret Book Co., 1954), pp. 7–8.

"Five Lessons of Love" by Elaine Cannon, from *Mothering* (Salt Lake City: Bookcraft, 1993), pp. 43–45.

"'That's All Right'" by Brookie Peterson, from *A Woman's Hope* (Salt Lake City: Bookcraft, 1991), p. 62.

"Christmas Story" by Kathleen "Casey" Null, from Kathleen "Casey" Null and Carolyn Sessions Allen, *From Here to Maternity* (Salt Lake City: Bookcraft, 1987), pp. 98–100.

"The Daffodil Principle" by Jaroldeen Asplund Edwards, from *Celebration! Ten Principles of More Joyous Living* (Salt Lake City: Deseret Book Co., 1995), pp. 39–44, 48–49.

Children

"He Still Had His Old Ones" by Michaelene P. Grassli, from *What I Have Learned from Children* (Salt Lake City: Deseret Book Co., 1993), p. 60.

"'I Always Do That'" by Sherrie Johnson, from *Spiritually Centered Motherhood* (Salt Lake City: Bookcraft, 1983), p. 33.

"Stature" by Vesta Nickerson Fairbairn, *Relief Society Magazine,* September 1966, p. 680.

"'Is the Book of Mormon True?'" by Michaelene P. Grassli, from *What I Have Learned from Children* (Salt Lake City: Deseret Book Co., 1993), pp. 28–29.

"'I Love You to Infinity'" by George D. Durrant, from *The Art of*

Raising Parents: A Young Person's Guide (Salt Lake City. Bookcraft, 1977), p. 88.

"Dear Primary Teacher" by Kathleen "Casey" Null, from Kathleen "Casey" Null and Carolyn Sessions Allen, *From Here to Maternity* (Salt Lake City: Bookcraft, 1987), pp. 21, 23.

"Music to the Ears" by Francine R. Bennion, from "Come unto Him, to Joy and Peace," in *Behold Your Little Ones,* ed. Barbara B. Smith and Shirley W. Thomas (Salt Lake City: Bookcraft, 1999), p. 45.

"'Listen to Me'" by Marilyn Jeppson Choules, from "Kindness to Be Counted On," in *Behold Your Little Ones,* ed. Barbara B. Smith and Shirley W. Thomas (Salt Lake City: Bookcraft, 1999), p. 98.

"'Of Course We've Seen Him!'" by Michaelene P. Grassli, from *What I Have Learned from Children* (Salt Lake City: Deseret Book Co., 1993), p. 24.

"Confection Perfectionist" by Kathleen "Casey" Null, from Kathleen "Casey" Null and Carolyn Sessions Allen, *From Here to Maternity* (Salt Lake City: Bookcraft, 1987), pp. 95–98.

Husbands and Fathers

"What Love Is" by Janene Wolsey Baadsgaard, from *Is There Life After Birth?* (Salt Lake City: Deseret Book Co., 1983), pp. 25–28.

"A Father's Support" by Anita R. Canfield, from *By Small and Simple Things* (Salt Lake City: Bookcraft, 1999), pp 60–62.

"'Plant Onions'" by Marion D. Hanks, from *Bread Upon the Waters* (Salt Lake City: Bookcraft, 1991), pp. 293–94.

"Serving Mother" by Marilyn Jeppson Choules, from "Kindness to Be Counted On," in *Behold Your Little Ones,* ed. Barbara B. Smith and Shirley W. Thomas (Salt Lake City: Bookcraft, 1999), p. 100.

"Little Wrangles" by Edgar A. Guest, from *When Day Is Done* (Chicago: The Reilly and Lee Co., 1921), pp. 127–28.

"Drastic Measures" by Janene Wolsey Baadsgaard, from *Is There Life After Birth?* (Salt Lake City: Deseret Book Co., 1983), pp. 21–22.

"'I Heard You'" by Anita R. Canfield, from *A Perfect Brightness of Hope* (Salt Lake City: Deseret Book Co., 1991), pp. 78–79.

"The Decision" by Marion D. Hanks, from *Bread Upon the Waters* (Salt Lake City: Bookcraft, 1991), pp. 234–35.

"Ah, Alone!" by Kathleen "Casey" Null, from Kathleen "Casey" Null and Carolyn Sessions Allen, *From Here to Maternity* (Salt Lake City: Bookcraft, 1987), pp. 42–43.

Struggle and Sacrifice

"Church Time" by Janene Wolsey Baadsgaard, from *Why Does My Mother's Day Potted Plant Always Die?* (Salt Lake City: Deseret Book Co., 1988), pp. 6–8.

"Was It Worth It? A Letter to My Wife, Marilyn" by George D. Durrant, from *Mother, Our Heavenly Connection* (Salt Lake City: Bookcraft, 1984), pp. 49–62.

"Just for a Change" by Susan Noyes Anderson, © 1996 by Susan D. (Noyes) Anderson, from *At the End of Your Rope, There's Hope: Parenting Teens in Crisis* (Salt Lake City: Deseret Book Co., 1997), pp. 59–60.

"'Get Used to It'" by Karen J. Ashton, from "Happiness Intended," in *Behold Your Little Ones,* ed. Barbara B. Smith and Shirley W. Thomas (Salt Lake City: Bookcraft, 1999), pp. 60–61.

"The Red Silk Dress" by Ardeth G. Kapp, from *What Latter-day*

Stripling Warriors Learn from Their Mothers (Salt Lake City: Deseret Book Co., 1996), pp. 47–51.

"'Do You Think That I Don't Love You?'" by LaDawn A. Jacob, from "Strengthening Our Nurturing Natures," in *Every Good Thing: Talks from the 1997 BYU Women's Conference,* ed. Dawn Hall Anderson, Susette Fletcher Green, and Dlora Hall Dalton (Salt Lake City: Deseret Book Co., 1998), pp. 179–80.

"Mother Came First" by George D. Durrant, from *The Art of Raising Parents: A Young Person's Guide* (Salt Lake City: Bookcraft, 1977), p. 36.

"The Choice" by Wilford Woodruff, from *Leaves from My Journal* (Salt Lake City: Juvenile Instructor's Office, 1882), pp. 54–55.

"'Is William Going?'" by Leonard J. Arrington and Susan Arrington Madsen, from *Sunbonnet Sisters: True Stories of Mormon Women and Frontier Life* (Salt Lake City: Bookcraft, 1984), pp. 29–31.

"A Drink of Water" by Annie Pike Greenwood, *Young Woman's Journal,* March 1913, p. 147.

On the Lighter Side

"Perfecting Motherhood" by Kathleen "Casey" Null, from Kathleen "Casey" Null and Carolyn Sessions Allen, *From Here to Maternity* (Salt Lake City: Bookcraft, 1987), pp. 14–16.

"Mashed Potatoes" by Jane F. Hinckley, from Virginia H. Pearce, ed., *Glimpses into the Life and Heart of Marjorie Pay Hinckley* (Salt Lake City: Deseret Book Co., 1999), p. 141.

"The Real 'Facts of Life'" by Janene Wolsey Baadsgaard, from *Why Does My Mother's Day Potted Plant Always Die?* (Salt Lake City: Deseret Book Co., 1988), pp. 12–13.

"'Where Did She Come From?'" by Michaelene P. Grassli, from

What I Have Learned from Children (Salt Lake City: Deseret Book Co., 1993), pp. 25–26.

"Ghostly Visitors" by A. Gail Smith, from *Shadowfall: Reflections on Nurturing Family Values* (Salt Lake City: Deseret Book Co., 1996), pp. 29–31.

"'I Don't Think I'll Get Married in the Temple'" by Bette S. Molgard, from *Everyday Battles* (Salt Lake City: Bookcraft, 1999), p. 58.

"Mother's Day Shouldn't Be Guilt Day" by Kathleen "Casey" Null, from Kathleen "Casey" Null and Carolyn Sessions Allen, *From Here to Maternity* (Salt Lake City: Bookcraft, 1987), pp. 24–25.

"A Disarming Humor" by Kathleen H. Barnes, from Virginia H. Pearce, ed., *Glimpses into the Life and Heart of Marjorie Pay Hinckley* (Salt Lake City: Deseret Book Co., 1999), pp. 112–14.

"'A Mother for All Seasons?'" by Janene Wolsey Baadsgaard, from *Why Does My Mother's Day Potted Plant Always Die?* (Salt Lake City: Deseret Book Co., 1988), p. 131.

An Eternal Perspective

"Thinking of You" by Bertha A. Kleinman, *Relief Society Magazine,* April 1943, p. 296.

"'You're Like a Mother'" by Ardeth G. Kapp, from the compilation *LDS Women's Treasury: Insights and Inspiration for Today's Woman* (Salt Lake City: Deseret Book Co., 1997), pp. 155–61.

"A Change in Routine" by Kathleen "Casey" Null, from *Where Are We Going Besides Crazy?* (Salt Lake City: Bookcraft, 1989), pp. 57–58.

"David" by Udora Morris, *Relief Society Magazine,* December 1968, p. 899.

"A Family Is . . ." by Elaine Cannon, from *Life—One to a Customer* (Salt Lake City: Bookcraft, 1981), pp. 118–20.

"The Inevitable Evolution" by Carolyn Sessions Allen, from Kathleen "Casey" Null and Carolyn Sessions Allen, *From Here to Maternity* (Salt Lake City: Bookcraft, 1987), pp. 89–91.

"A Promise for Eternity" by Susan Noyes Anderson, © 1996 by Susan D. (Noyes) Anderson, from *At the End of Your Rope, There's Hope: Parenting Teens in Crisis* (Salt Lake City: Deseret Book Co., 1997), pp. 29–30.

"A Very Special Mission" by Carole Kirk, from Marilynne Todd Linford, *Give Mom a Standing Ovation* (Salt Lake City: Bookcraft, 1996), pp. 152–54.

"Celestial Love" by Brookie Peterson, from *A Woman's Hope* (Salt Lake City: Bookcraft, 1991), pp. 134–35.

"The Bridge Through the Mist" by Kathleen "Casey" Null, from Kathleen "Casey" Null and Carolyn Sessions Allen, *From Here to Maternity* (Salt Lake City: Bookcraft, 1987), pp. 104–5.